Growing
at Greenfields

Growing
at Greenfields

A seasonal guide to growing, eating
and creating from a beautiful Scottish garden

DIANA YATES

Contents

Introduction

The pivotal 'I can't go on like this' moment came to me in a Virgin Active car park in Johannesburg, South Africa, on a random Wednesday afternoon in the height of summer. I knew my 12-hour days as the COO of a large multinational corporation were numbered. I felt trapped, slightly manic and completely out of control. Life had become a cycle of long work days, even longer work trips, and late family dinners. I realized while I sat crying in my husband Andrew's arms in that car park, that even though I was a present mama when I was at home, I was living to work. Work consumed nearly my every waking thought, my immune system was shot, and the pace just seemed to be increasing. I'd fallen into my career without much thought about what I wanted from life and had got swept away with it all. Truth be told, I don't think I knew what I wanted in my early twenties when I set out into the working world. Hats off to anyone who does.

All I knew was that now, at 33, I was close to burnout. After the hypothetical, not-so-hypothetical, 'Are we actually going to do this?' series of conversations with Andrew, we decided to leave South Africa, where we had spent the last decade working as expats and raising our three children. It was a no-brainer to return home to the UK, but neither of us had a plan, or any idea as to what would come next.

Fast-forward a little and, after spending two happy if not completely settled years in Oxfordshire, Andrew and I decided to move close to where we had both grown up – nearer to family and back to village life in Scotland. It was December 2016, and while out for a wander around some local villages I caught a glimpse of a house surrounded by trees that I'd originally come across through an online property search.

Before even viewing the house, I knew without a shadow of uncertainty that it was where I wanted us to make a home. It was love at first sight;

perfectly nestled among mature trees, with tons of space for energetic children and their friends to run about. Thankfully Andrew didn't need much convincing, as he saw the potential too.

In May 2017, Greenfields, the over-budget beauty as it was, became ours, complete with an ancient boiler that would go pop just before our first Christmas, a couple of resident bats in our bedroom and a wild yet beautiful woodland garden. Oh, and in the autumn – 4,362,578 fallen leaves.

What people don't often say when they make the move from a highly convenient city life to the countryside is that there is a huge period of adjustment, even if you grew up in the countryside, like I did. There was a moment or, more truthfully, quite a number of 'Oh God' moments, when we looked at each other and said, 'What the heck have we done?' Usually these occurred while lying in bed sandwiched between hot-water bottles and a newly purchased tog-15 duvet on a particularly frigid night in a 240-year-old house with single-pane glass windows.

I wasn't immediately tuned into the slower pace. I missed the ease of a last-minute food delivery service, the buzz of the city at night and its lights, as well as having a reason to get dressed up every day. In all honesty it took me over a year to feel really settled, a year of experiencing Greenfields in every season, to feel truly at home, and a year to slow down, look up from my screen of choice and let in the stunning natural world that was always there but that I hadn't paid attention to before.

PART 1

---

*The Story
So Far*

Years One and Two

A decision had to be made very early on in our move to Greenfields, one that wasn't discussed at all during the 'rose-tinted spectacles' viewing phase. Who was going to look after the almost two-acre garden? I hadn't planned to start a journey towards 'the good life' before our move. Honestly, I hadn't given the garden much thought beyond who was going to cut the grass. I was not a gardener, so for the first few months, we found a local chap to pop in once a week with his lawnmower, while I occasionally looked on from over the edge of my laptop.

Roll on our first autumn and a last-minute decision to spend the day in the garden raking up the first huge drop of leaves. The air was crisp that day. Andrew had a campfire going, the kids were buzzing about helping to gather leaves and sticks for the fire. We kicked around a rugby ball, raked and picked up what felt like a few tonnes of leaves. By dusk we had cleared the large expanse of front garden. I remember walking across the lawn feeling an enormous sense of achievement, along with majorly aching muscles. The feeling that stayed with me, though, one that I now try to recreate often, was the overwhelming sense of peace that had soaked into my bones and filled me up with an unfamiliar sense of wellbeing and belonging. When was the last time I had felt such calm? I honestly could not remember.

Andrew and I wandered around the garden in the days that followed, discussing our initial thoughts for what then seemed to be an overwhelming space. How could we make it our own, and where would we begin?

In the end, the decision was made to start small, to focus on vegetables over flowers, and to fix immediate problems while maintaining what the garden was already blessed with – mainly mature trees, hedging and shrubs. The one thing we agreed on instantly was to view the garden as a space divided into different rooms, each with a different purpose and style. This approach helped us to focus on the various areas in terms of planting and maintenance, and also made the mammoth task in front of us appear much less daunting.

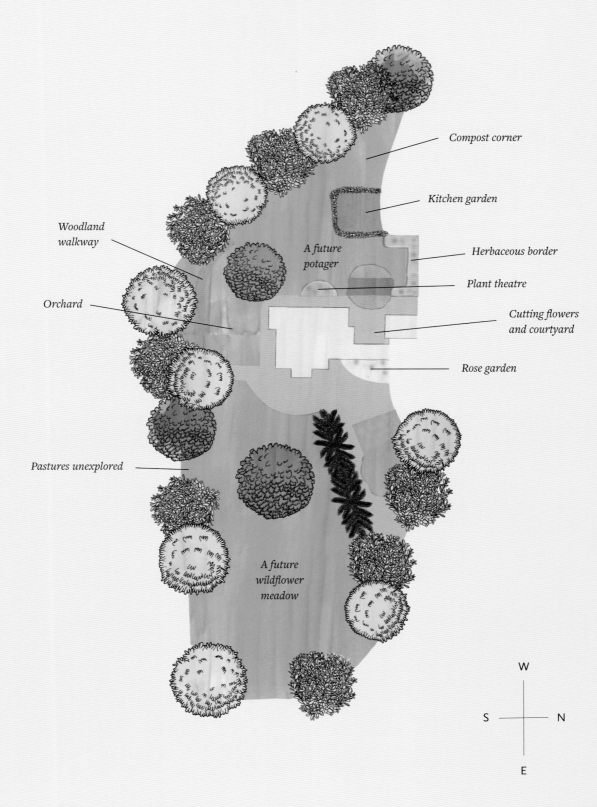

Compost corner

Kitchen garden

Herbaceous border

Woodland
walkway

A future
potager

Plant theatre

Cutting flowers
and courtyard

Orchard

Rose garden

Pastures unexplored

A future
wildflower
meadow

W

S ── N

E

The Kitchen Garden 2018

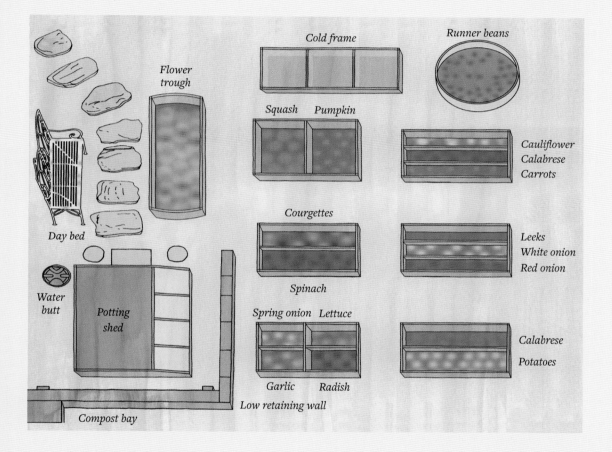

Flower trough

Cold frame

Runner beans

Squash   Pumpkin

Cauliflower
Calabrese
Carrots

Day bed

Courgettes

Leeks
White onion
Red onion

Water butt

Potting shed

Spinach

Spring onion   Lettuce

Calabrese

Potatoes

Garlic   Radish

Low retaining wall

Compost bay

Aerial sketches of the garden highlighting the structure and our plans as they were in early 2018, along with projects such as the potager and plant theatre that came later, and unexplored areas to be developed in future years. As the saying goes, a garden is never complete, and what could be more exciting than that?

Creating the kitchen garden

Being a beginner at all things horticultural, setting up the kitchen garden was a steep learning curve, and overwhelming at times, but I relished the opportunity to learn something new; something so completely detached from the life I was living before. Decisions included whether or not to level the slope of the kitchen garden, to plant into raised beds or the ground, to install a greenhouse or shed. There were discussions about what was the ideal distance between each bed, what material should be used on the walkways, and what type of soil would be best for everything we wanted to grow. See opposite, top, for a rather bleak before shot of what would become the kitchen garden.

My first winter was spent huddled with my children and husband in the one warmish room in the house, watching reruns of *Beechgrove* and *Gardeners' World*, and devouring gardening blogs online. While doing so, I had a thought to set up my own gardening blog to document our journey, in the hope of meeting other gardeners who might share their knowledge with me.

My online searches invariably led to more questions – such as dig or no dig, and what are the best methods of sowing? It was a whole new world! I was excited for spring but I knew there was a lot of infrastructure to set up before we could even get to the planting stage. The fenced-off area behind the inherited beech hedge seemed like the least overwhelming place to start, being self-contained and pretty much a blank slate. If it all went wrong, we decided, we could shut the gate and try again the following year.

After much research, I went for a soil mix for the raised beds of one third compost, one third well-rotted manure and one third topsoil. If planting direct in your garden's native soil, I recommend purchasing a soil test kit, which will tell you what type you have and what is needed to improve its drainage and fertility.

The two main approaches to gardening are the 'dig' and 'no dig' methods. The no dig method allows the soil to retain its structure, as it is not dug at any stage. Soil amendments such as compost or mulch are added on top of the soil only. Weeds are suppressed rather than hoed or pulled. In contrast, the dig method is the traditional way of forking over the soil in preparation for planting, usually in spring, while adding soil improvers. I allow the crop to dictate the method. For example, I may use a fork to dig out potatoes or pull weeds by hand, but I won't till or turn the soil before planting. In time you will find what method works best for you and your garden.

The rest of the answers to my burning questions were summed up in my second blog post – see page 16 and the tips on pages 18–19.

Kitchen garden stats

Full sun and south-facing

•

9 metres by 9 metres
(30 feet by 30 feet)

•

Gradually sloped site

•

Fenced and gated

•

Bordered by a mature beech hedge
and original stone wall

•

Height above sea level
262 metres (860 feet)

Extract from the blog, 15 April 2018

The spot behind the beech hedge has already become somewhat of an oasis over the past few weeks. Even the process of hard landscaping the area has been nothing short of therapeutic, especially when the sun shone. Needless to say, as a beginner I'm just learning the benefits of gardening; and I'm thoroughly enjoying the stress-free moments I find among the soil. I'm looking forward to retreating to the kitchen garden in the summer months to potter and ponder and, most of all, harvest, but before then we have got work to do!

The site for the kitchen garden was established by the previous owners and is absolutely the best spot, with generous amounts of sunshine and a south-facing aspect. At 81 square metres (872 square feet), I wanted to create a space that I could 'grow' into over the next few years. A space that will eventually fully sustain a family of five with vegetables and possibly fruit.

In the past two months, the plot has been levelled-ish, raised beds have been built and set in place, gravel has been poured on top of pinned landscape fabric and the potting shed is up. But before we get to the detail of all that, I wanted to share the plans for the space and, more importantly, what I hope to be growing very soon!

Initially, I wanted to stick with the original layout of four beds around the outside of the plot with a feature of some sort in the middle. Once we began the hard landscaping, I quickly realized this wouldn't be practical as the kitchen garden is at the top of a fairly steep slope and not close to the garage or any storage, so I needed a space on the plot to store tools. In addition, I wanted to make use of the south-facing aspect so I could start seeds off undercover.

I also toyed with the idea of a water feature in the centre, but I didn't necessarily want to attract birds to the veg patch or midges, for that matter!

There wasn't anything necessarily wrong with the soil, but the idea of raised beds really appealed to me for ease and soil development – plus, they look good! I opted for a potting shed with huge slanted windows to make the most of the intermittent sun, to store tools and as a place I could escape to with a cup of tea every now and then.

I'll install a rainwater butt off the back of the shed, which will hopefully provide enough water for the plot without the need to have irrigation brought up the hill. We may end up adding a tap and hose at some point.

Although we've made plans to create a compost corner at the far top of the garden, I have also included a compost bay inside the plot, which I'm aiming to make cheaply out of pallets, specifically for the kitchen garden. The total garden is a very generous size and the back portion is on a slope, so creating self-contained areas wherever possible can only help us manage it better in the long run.

So yes, not rocket science but I think we are making the most of what we have without overcrowding things. I have left almost a metre between the beds to make moving around them with the wheelbarrow a doddle. I also envisage little pots at the end of beds filled with companion plants, herbs and bursts of colour.

Lessons learned

Fast-forward to July 2019, after a full year of growing in the kitchen garden. Here are some of the key things that I learned.

1.   If it doesn't germinate, try again or purchase seedlings. You are no less of a gardener if you grow everything from seedlings/plugs bought from the garden centre rather than seeds. Gardening should be stress-free. The veg or flowers won't judge you, I promise!

2.   Preparation is key. I cannot tell you how many times I've looked back at my sowing, feeding and harvesting table that I put together back in April. It's become my quick reference guide when I can't remember when or how much to feed the courgettes or to know when my potatoes are ready to harvest, and it keeps me on track with my to-do list.

To create a handy reference guide for your garden, make notes under the headings below for each vegetable (or flower) you decide to grow.

Variety
Companion plant
When to sow
Final position
Care
Fertilizer
Harvest

3.   Take photos to track growth. Once everything is in the ground, growth takes off at a ridiculous rate. It's really nice to have photos of the progress over the growing cycle, to see how far things have come and how they change. I use my mobile phone to take all my garden pics, then save everything to a separate photo album on my phone so I can easily go back and reference them – like a visual journal, if you will.

4.   You don't need all the tools to get started. If you're just starting out with a veg or flower patch, there is a fair bit of equipment to get, and costs can mount quickly. But you can make do with just a few essential tools until the budget allows. For me, these were a metal soil rake I already had, which I used as a tiller and hoe as well as a rake – if you turn it onto its side you can also create your sowing drills with it. Labels, labels and more labels (the little wooden lollipop sticks are perfect and cost only pennies), a trowel, a spade and a watering can with a fine rose for your seedlings indoors and a larger rose for outdoor watering. (See page 42 for a complete list.)

5.   Don't compare your plant growth or seedling progress to that of anyone else. At the beginning of spring, I realized that here in Scotland we would be trailing at least four weeks behind the rest of the UK in terms of growth. The daffodils had nearly come and gone down south by the time ours had arrived. In the height of summer, gardens in the same village are at varying stages to mine. Your garden will do its thing in its own good time.

6.   Don't plan holidays when nearly everything is due to be harvested. Well, unless you want to miss it, of course, or spend your holiday worrying it will all go to seed before you get home.

7.   Wait a full growing year before you get stuck into a new garden. This is quite difficult when you're impatient to get started, but it's worth it in the end. While you wait, catalogue the plants and flowers and decide what to keep or move.

8.   And if you don't like it, turf it. It can seem quite callous to turf a mature plant, but it's you that has to look at it every day. To ease the guilt, you could transplant it to a less conspicuous place or donate it to a friend or neighbour.

9.   Sweet peas sown in April will not germinate. Next time I will stick to the winter sowing schedule recommended by the cutting garden queen herself, Sarah Raven. (See page 166 for a sweet pea sowing guide.)

10.   Experiments prevent perfectionism. This has really helped me in avoiding the desire to try to make everything perfect. I planted five potatoes in a pot, which deep down I knew was not big enough, just to see what happened. The end result? As expected, lots of little potatoes!

11. **If in doubt, ask for help.** The gardening community is one of the friendliest I've come across in real life, Instagram and on my blog. People are keen to share their knowledge – and their seeds.

12. **Gardening is addictive.** From seeing the first of your seeds sprout to eating your home-grown vegetables is a deeply rewarding experience!

The same view of the kitchen garden, seven weeks apart.

Top tips for setting up a raised bed garden

1

If choosing raised beds, opt for no more than 1m (3 feet) wide, so you can easily access the middle of the bed without stretching.

2

The higher the raised bed the better for your back, and the easier it will be to maintain. A minimum of 35–54cm (14–21 inches) high caters for the longest-growing root crops – unless you are aiming for champion produce for the show bench!

3

Leave at least 70–100cm (2–3 feet) between beds for ease of movement with a wheelbarrow, and for dotting pots about to maximize the growing space.

4

If you are gardening on a gradual slope, I don't believe levelling the beds fully is totally needed but if your garden is falling on more of a gradient, take the time to dig out a flat base so the beds can sit levelled on all sides. This will help prevent rainwater run-off later.

5

When using reclaimed older wood, double-check it has not been chemically treated with CCA (chromated copper arsenate). This chemical, which is toxic to humans, was officially removed from the market in 2003. However, some previously treated wood may still be in circulation – especially if it is reclaimed.

6

Raised beds can be built quite successfully from old wooden pallets. There are plenty of online tutorials that lay out the process step by step. Just make sure the pallets have an HT (heat-treated) stamp mark and not the MB (methyl bromide) mark, as this chemical is toxic and may leach into your plants. I would also avoid pallets with no markings at all, just to be safe.

7

Droughts are becoming more frequent during the growing season, so having a way to collect rainwater will benefit your garden greatly. Rainwater has a slightly acidic pH, which your soil will appreciate. Soil that runs slightly on the acidic side will use up more of the nutrients available when fertilized.

Year Three

The first two years of growing at Greenfields were sweet success granted by long beautiful summers and an abundance of motivation to continually learn new skills. By the end of my second growing season, the positive impacts from gardening had infiltrated every area of my life, and more specifically my outlook on life. The unfulfilled manic version of me no longer existed. I now worked to live and filled my down time with soul-nurturing projects, experimenting with preserving and preparing recipes to make the most of our home-grown produce. I taught myself to sew, and every day spent time nurturing this other new hobby, which later would become so much more.

During the spring and summer months I would rise early, and often be in the garden at sun up, just enjoying the quiet. I was happy within myself and felt an inner peace I had never known. For the first time in my life I didn't want anything, except to be part of all of the little moments and big moments of my children's lives, and to soak up all nature had to offer, in every season. The garden gave abundantly, and the scarce insect population – an ongoing topic of conversation during our first summer here – was no more. The garden was buzzing and so was I.

Then 2020 began in the shadow of the Covid-19 pandemic and redundancy for both Andrew and me just a few months before, when the company we worked for went under. I decided to turn my sewing hobby into a fully fledged business a month before the pandemic hit. I know, what great timing! Little did I know how dark times would become for my family just as the garden woke up for spring.

As the first lockdown began, so had the seed sowing in earnest. The kids each chose a crop to grow and we spent happy hours together sowing and potting on in the greenhouse. Time ticked by wonderfully slowly. My elder daughter Mia made a herb garden in containers, my younger daughter Georgia started off courgettes and planted new potatoes in grow bags. My son and youngest child, Joseph, who could be found with me in the garden the most, helped to sow carrots, planted out onions and dug holes with his dad for our latest garden project for growing vegetables – a potager.

April was unseasonably warm, filled with sunshine and afternoons after homeschooling spent cloud-spotting lying on the grass. Most days Andrew and I would work on the potager while the kids swung too high on the tree swing, played chase with the dogs or rolled down the hill giggling all the while. It was ridiculously idyllic.

I remember numerous conversations with Andrew about how fortunate we felt, because the kids could hop over the fence and wander up over the hill behind our home if they were feeling stir crazy under lockdown conditions. Even though we were anxious over the future, with income dwindling and a large mortgage to pay, there was still an overriding sense of calm, as Andrew was in the early days of job hunting and ultimately there was very little we had control over. What would be, would be – there was nothing to be done, as the whole world had shut down.

We lived in our restricted bubble, trying to minimize our consumption of any external source of news for a total of 45 days. During that time I drew out a simple nine-bed potager on the ground, to allow us to expand our edible growing space and make space for a cut-flower garden. Andrew and I marked out the beds with a string line and spray, then spent a solid week digging out and levelling each bed. At that point no one knew how long the pandemic would last, but as a couple we had a project, something to ground us in between those moments of panic.

The beds were topped with a compost and topsoil mix and bordered with bare-root box hedging. The work was hard on the back but extremely satisfying for the mind.

It was on one of those 'normal' lockdown days when our 10-year-old son Joseph died. A freak accident while playing took him from us suddenly and traumatically. Our lives fell apart.

The longer story is that life will never be the same; we continue to navigate each day as best we can, and we aim to live life the way our boy did, with purpose and big dreams. The shorter story is that the garden saved us that summer. The hours and days that followed were a fog; still in lockdown at the height of the tightest restrictions, my family and I were reeling. Days came and went on autopilot, while I was battered back and forth between shock, denial and utter desolation.

Those early days were the longest and darkest of my life. Andrew and I stayed close to our daughters, with mind-numbing TV in the background, holding each other and talking. At times my husband and I would sit quietly together in the kitchen garden and cry. At others, we would talk, and talk, and talk, trying to make sense of it all, trying to answer the unanswerable question, why?

It was during one of those quiet moments in the garden that I noticed the first of the carrot seeds had begun to germinate. Joseph's seeds. I'd never been so happy and so agonized to see seedlings grow, but the power of nature picked me up that day and hasn't let me go since, because they would need thinning and watering. Someone had to look after them. The intangible thread of sowing, planting, feeding and harvesting pulled me forward mentally and emotionally while I grieved, and while the process of nurturing seedlings sown by my son's hands in a way helped a little to fill the void of no longer being able to nurture him.

I will never forget the summer of 2020, for how unnaturally noisy and silent it was at the same time. The skies were unmarred by the sounds or white lines made by aeroplanes, the roads were empty of cars. Instead, birdsong was louder than ever before, and the sheep in the field next door joined the chorus, along with the steady hum of bees all summer long. The summer went on and my husband, girls and I continued to put one foot in front of the other.

The potager was a peaceful and productive addition to the garden. As well as jugs and jugs of fresh cut flowers for the house, the new beds gave a large yield of potatoes, peas and parsnips. I decided to dedicate one bed to asparagus, a long-lasting perennial vegetable. Patience is key when choosing a spot for the tender spears, as you'll only begin reaping the rewards from crops produced in the third year. Onions, however, were not a success, as it turns out they don't like to be blown about in the wind. Lesson learned.

By early autumn, I wasn't ready to leave the garden behind. Grief was weighing heavy on me and I needed the mindful distraction of garden chores to quieten my thoughts when it all became too much. Andrew was suffering similarly and relished the task of revamping the overgrown rockery – also known as the view from the kitchen sink. He worked tirelessly moving around large rocks to create a terraced garden, and so started the creation of the plant theatre.

The potager complete with obelisks for height and a central stone bird bath
to ground the space and encourage wildlife.

The progress of the potager

(spring and summer 2020)

Garden stats

Full sun and south-facing

•

*15 metres by 9 metres
(50 feet by 30 feet)*

•

Gradually sloped site

•

Exposed

The plant theatre

At the time, I decided to leave the shrubs alongside the plant theatre/container garden to see how they would work together as the seasons changed. Eventually, almost two years later, I removed the azalea shrub right in the middle. Once that was rehomed, the space became more open, allowing me to see its full potential. I wish I had moved it sooner! As time has gone on, moss has regrown over the stones, adding another lovely texture to each display. There have been lots of valuable lessons learned over the past couple of years – what works together and what we should avoid.

Here are my top tips if you're creating something similar in your garden.

Step width Bear in mind the width of your steps in relation to the diameter of the largest pot you have or could potentially have sitting on them. Will it fit?

Pot choice Pots should be frostproof and robust, because you won't be moving them all indoors in winter. I use a mixture of galvanized metal, glazed ceramic and terracotta, and I try to choose colours that won't compete with the flowers grown in them.

A note on colour I aim for fillers that are pretty in their own right but also help to make a cohesive display. In the display opposite I've used a mixture of forget-me-nots, nemesia and narcissi to give a sense of continuity.

Choose great perennials Hostas, heucheras, aquilegia, forget-me-nots, euphorbia, ferns, certain tulip varieties, daffodils, nepeta, rosemary, lavender, nemesia, grasses.

Plant pretty annuals Pansies, violas, osteospermum, smaller dahlia varieties, cosmos, phlox, calendula, nasturtiums.

Make it edible Growing in containers is an excellent option for smaller garden spaces. Instead of using foliage plants such as hostas or heucheras for 'rest spots' for the eye, consider using edibles such as lettuces, rosemary, chives, thyme, potatoes, parsley and mint, which are all great options for container growing.

LEFT *The first display in autumn 2020, a little too spread out but it had the desired effect of lifting my spirits every time I walked past or looked out of the kitchen window, and for that I was grateful.*
OPPOSITE *I learned that grouping the pots closer together and using filler plants would add impact to a display.*

The rockery before, spring 2018.

The plant theatre starting to take shape, early autumn 2020.

Andrew placing stones to form the steps, early autumn 2020.

Weed membrane and pea gravel was laid to finish the theatre, early autumn 2020.

Year Four

The following year was mostly spent trying to navigate a path through the ever-changing facets of grief, while trying to heal our hearts and minds. Garden therapy played a huge part in helping me work through the trauma. Observing nature and the seasonal cycles is unrivalled in its power to keep the body and mind moving forward. My daughters were my focus and my reason to keep getting out of bed every day, and striving to create beautiful spaces in the garden for us all to enjoy when I wasn't sewing gave me purpose and head space.

While the outside world was still mostly restricted in some way or another, I decided the growing season ahead was going to be dedicated to nurturing bountiful crops and creating beautiful borders filled to the brim with colour. And it just so happened to be the year that I was asked to write a book about my gardening journey. So this is where I leave part one of the story to take you through a full year, season by season, of growing at Greenfields. I have included some of my favourite family recipes, handy for using up any home-grown produce gluts, along with ideas for using flowers in creative ways. Living seasonally is a way of life I have come to treasure, and nurturing a garden has ultimately given me an immeasurable amount in return.

'To plant a garden is to believe in tomorrow.'
AUDREY HEPBURN

PART 2

———

A Year
at Greenfields

Spring

Spring in my step

Living a life that centres around nature and the seasons in terms of food, creativity, simple observations and pace is truly the most transformative thing ever to happen to me. There is no other way to explain it. The rewards are both intangible, tangible, endless and bountiful. From the first sign of seedlings appearing above the soil, or the first courgette forming, to a border filled with flowers all grown from seed, or a cold store filled with harvests to see your family through the winter months, there is truly nothing more rewarding. These days, I wait with bated breath for the earliest indication that the shift towards spring has begun. Snowdrops may be a late winter flower, but the emergence of these flowers is also the first sign that spring is on the horizon, in my book, and so the anticipation begins.

The steady succession that follows reminds me of Vivaldi's *Four Seasons*, specifically, 'Spring 1', as recomposed by Max Richter – a good one to play on repeat at this time of year. After the snowdrops, a purple carpet of crocuses appears across the lawn, followed by the simple daffodil – or narcissus, if you prefer – in every shape and form along the woodland walkway. Then come the tulips, tulips and more tulips in beds and pots. The English bluebells are next, by far the best naturalizer in my garden. They will pop up in hybrid form, too, often pink and more rarely in white. My favourite forget-me-nots are hot on their heels, which now signify an extremely difficult time of the year for my family, but at the same time offer comfort with their enduring nature and delicate beauty. The cow parsley then seems to gently waft me into summer, with large swathes planted in the meadow areas of the garden between tall grasses. The arrival of spring blooms may vary by up to four weeks year on year, with varying weather patterns, but inevitably spring will arrive and undoubtedly bring hope, motivation and a renewed sense of purpose along with it.

In my quest for plant knowledge, I discovered many varieties of narcissi; there are literally thousands of them. I will share more on my top picks in the autumn chapter, how to plant them and some of my other favourite bulbs, but for now it's time to focus on getting the garden ready for the busiest season of the year.

The beginner gardener's toolkit

Andrew and I had very little when we first started out – a spade, trowel, soil rake, watering can and wheelbarrow were pretty much all we owned for the first year. Since then I've added some new tools that I now wouldn't be without.

Essentials

Bypass hand pruners For cutting flowers and harvesting vegetables, to pruning green shrubs with stems of 1cm (½ inch) thickness or less.

Dutch hoe I often weed by hand, but this is my go-to tool for covering large areas, allowing you to cut the tops off weeds quickly before gathering them up.

Garden diary I use a bullet journal as my garden diary; the grid system is perfect for sketching plans to scale.

Horticultural fleece Great to pull out in a pinch for an unexpected frost or to raise the soil temperature of a raised bed a little earlier.

Long-handled spade It's a good idea to check the spade against your height, and check the weight of the spade to make sure you are picking the best one for you. Your back will thank you later.

Marker pen or chalk Look for a marker pen designed for plant labels, which will not fade in the sun.

Plant labels Slate, wood or reusable plastic are all fine.

Rainwater butt or trough If you're growing anything, you'll need a water source. Rainwater is better for plants, plus it's far better for the environment not to get the hose out if you can avoid it.

Root trainers For starting off seeds with longer root systems such as sweet peas, beans and sweetcorn.

Seed starting trays or pots Almost anything can be used as a seed tray or pot; an old biscuit tin, a length of guttering, empty kitchen paper and toilet rolls, yoghurt pots, milk cartons, juice jugs… The list is endless. Just make sure you pierce a few drainage holes into the bottom of the container. If traditional pots are more your style, there is a variety of materials to consider: bamboo, coir, terracotta, galvanized tin or heavy-duty, recycled plastic.

Soil rake Frequently used in the garden when applying mulch, levelling borders or flipped over to create drills for seed sowing.

Tine rake/leaf rake For easy leaf collection.

Trowel Perfect for smaller jobs such as planting out seedlings, transplanting perennials or potting up containers.

Watering can with a removable fine rose You will need the fine rose for seedlings and a larger rose for everything else.

Wheelbarrow or trolley Both are great options. If opting for a trolley, make sure it comes with a brake and tipping functionality. For smaller gardens, a pop-up bag is very handy and folds up small for storage.

Not essentials, but excellent to have especially if you live in an area with a shorter growing season, and would like to extend it by starting off seeds indoors:

Grow lights These mimic natural light, preventing leggy seedlings, and are often used to provide additional light to seeds started off indoors.

Propagator A mini greenhouse for your seedlings, often bought as a kit including a seed tray and domed lid to prevent seedlings drying out. Electric propagators provide a small amount of heat to the base of the seed tray, which can help to speed up seed germination.

The spring garden

Planning for the year ahead

Whether your growing space spans acres, is a compact courtyard or a bijou balcony garden, creating a plan of what you want to grow and where is an excellent place to start to gather your thoughts and determine what you would like to achieve from the growing season.

During this stage I like to begin by looking back at what did well and what didn't. Often I'll refer to my garden diary or photo journal for notes on areas to change and improve, along with previous years' planting plans.

In my garden, my aim is to cultivate different garden rooms for different purposes, so I will keep that in mind when deciding on plant style and placement. At the end of the day, though, there are no rules; your garden is your canvas. If you want to create a one-colour display made up of purple cabbage, alliums and lavender, then why not? As long as whatever you decide to grow is given the right conditions to produce healthy productive plants, your garden will thrive!

There is a certain feeling that comes from drawing a garden plan, even if you are not Picasso. The mindful time spent sketching out ideas, possibly adding colour to illustrate your garden palette, is something I have come to appreciate and look forward to over the winter. I stretch out this process now to work on it during the dreariest and coldest of days; curled up on the sofa, with colour pencils, a sketch pad, a cosy fire and the dog for company.

I start by drawing a sketch of each growing space, including raised beds, borders, larger pots, the greenhouse, potager and the south border. I fill in what crops and flowers I'd like to grow, being mindful of final planting distances between varieties and how many of each plant will therefore fit the space.

In the kitchen garden particularly, I will make sure I am rotating crops to minimize disease, and planting vegetables, herbs and flowers alongside their favourite companions to deter predators naturally. (See page 108 for more on natural pest control.)

Keep a little growing space (or a lot!) up your sleeve, for when you receive 'unsolicited' mail from your favourite garden nurseries tempting you with all the pretty things. This happens to me often during early spring, and before I know what's happened, I have parcels of extra seeds and plants arriving at the door! Each year, I like to try a couple of new varieties to experiment with, be it vegetables, herbs or flowers from bulb or seed. The plant kingdom is too vast not to keep on discovering new plants.

The choice about what to grow can on its own be overwhelming. One way to overcome this is to start by growing what you eat. Sounds obvious enough, right? But it's easy to get caught up in trending varieties currently winning in the popularity stakes rather than what will end up on the dinner table or be adored in a floral arrangement. In terms of ornamental plants, I often thumb through gardening catalogues and jot down blooms that catch my eye. A meander through the garden centre is also likely to produce a similar list.

Once I have a fairly definitive list, checking my seed storage tin is next. Old seed past its expiry date is less likely to give successful germination, but that doesn't mean you can't try them and see. I organize my seeds by sowing month, and once sown I move them on to the next month to remind me to sow a successional crop, so that there is always something to pick. The seed packet will often indicate the months in which the variety can be sown successfully, taking into consideration how long the crop or plant will take to mature.

*Purple sprouting broccoli, sown in May and planted out eight weeks later,
will be ready for picking from February onwards.*

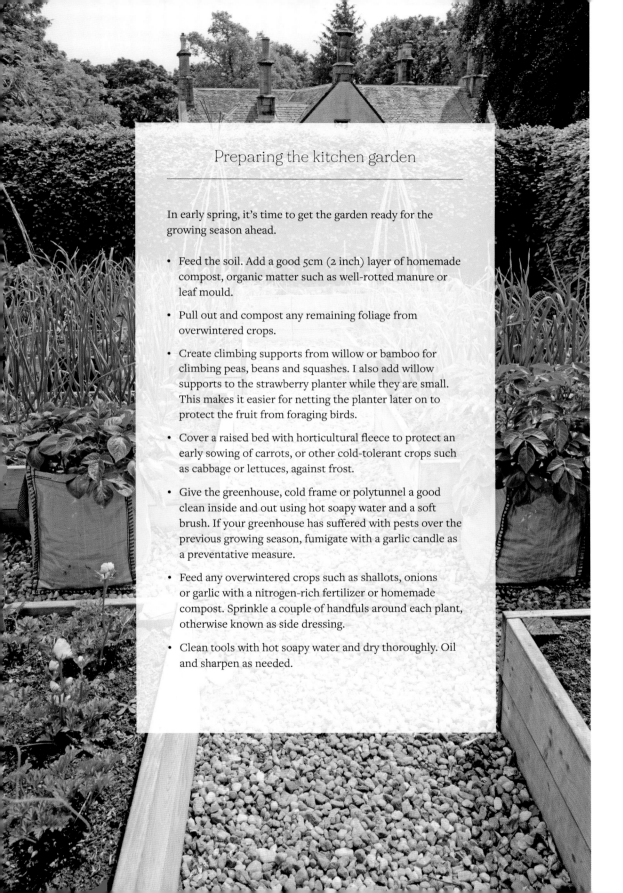

Preparing the kitchen garden

In early spring, it's time to get the garden ready for the growing season ahead.

- Feed the soil. Add a good 5cm (2 inch) layer of homemade compost, organic matter such as well-rotted manure or leaf mould.

- Pull out and compost any remaining foliage from overwintered crops.

- Create climbing supports from willow or bamboo for climbing peas, beans and squashes. I also add willow supports to the strawberry planter while they are small. This makes it easier for netting the planter later on to protect the fruit from foraging birds.

- Cover a raised bed with horticultural fleece to protect an early sowing of carrots, or other cold-tolerant crops such as cabbage or lettuces, against frost.

- Give the greenhouse, cold frame or polytunnel a good clean inside and out using hot soapy water and a soft brush. If your greenhouse has suffered with pests over the previous growing season, fumigate with a garlic candle as a preventative measure.

- Feed any overwintered crops such as shallots, onions or garlic with a nitrogen-rich fertilizer or homemade compost. Sprinkle a couple of handfuls around each plant, otherwise known as side dressing.

- Clean tools with hot soapy water and dry thoroughly. Oil and sharpen as needed.

Seed-sowing guide

Where and when you start off your seeds depends on the growing conditions in your area, the environment you can provide, the length of your growing season and how much space you have. It sounds like a lot to get right, but the seed packet will guide you on the majority of what you need to know, then experimenting and the guide set out on these next few pages will help you with the rest!

Light and warmth Making sure your seedlings have the right amount of light is crucial to growing strong healthy seedlings. For most a south-facing window is the perfect spot to start off seeds within the warmth of the house. If this is not possible, adding supplemental lighting will give your seedlings the additional light needed that the shorter days early in the growing season don't provide. A greenhouse or polytunnel will give seedlings the most natural light available.

Moisture To stop your seeds drying out before they have germinated, pop a propagation lid or humidity dome on top of the seed tray or pots once sown and watered to keep out air and create a humid environment. I usually keep the lid on until around 80 per cent of the seeds have sprouted before removing the lid completely to allow air and oxygen to circulate.

Airflow As well as light and warmth, seedlings need oxygen and good airflow. For seedlings started indoors, I set up a fan to aid circulation. A gentle breeze will help seedlings to become stronger and more robust over time. Gently brush your fingers over the seedlings a couple of times per day to achieve the same effect without electricity.

Sowing quantities It is very easy to get carried away with seed sowing, especially when starting off seeds in trays for pricking out later. But do you actually need 10 tomato plants of the same variety, just because the seed packet contains 10? I try to limit myself to sowing one or two extra than I'll need just in case I lose one along the way, and then any extra seeds or seedlings are shared with friends and family or donated to community seed swaps. On the other hand, when sowing flowers for borders, I aim for much larger quantities; being able to create drifts with annuals makes for a more impactful display.

When to sow Knowledge of the average last frost date in your area coupled with the information on the seed packet is pretty much all you need to decide on when to sow. I'll also take a look at the forecast for any extreme dips in temperature to make sure I won't have to nip back and forth to the greenhouse in arctic conditions to check on seedlings! Starting off seeds earlier than recommended may sound like a good idea to get a head start, but often germinating seeds is actually the easiest part of the process. Thereafter providing your seedlings with enough light and warmth – particularly earlier on in the growing season – is quite a bit trickier to maintain. So being patient at this stage, though often easier said than done, will benefit your garden in the long run.

During my first year of growing, the only space with any warmth and decent light in my garden was the potting shed, so I began all of my seeds in there with lots of enthusiasm and very little knowledge. At times the shed would overheat and the seedlings would dry out and wither, before rebounding after a good soak and a prayer! Long story short, seedlings are mostly tough little things. I still had bumper crops of vegetables and the majority survived. As time goes on I continue to tweak the growing conditions in the hope of improving yields and results.

Let's use tender chillies as an example, as these are always the first seeds I start off in late winter (late January or early February) due to their long growing season and the fact they are most averse to the Scottish climate. They need tropical temperatures and full sun to thrive, which are both rarely found for any length of time in my area. My greenhouse is unheated, which means it can hover around freezing or just below for weeks over winter and early spring.

So my best option is to start them off indoors where the temperature ranges from 18 to 20°C (64 to 68°F). To prevent seedlings becoming leggy and to make sure they remain strong and healthy, I place them under grow lights. Once the greenhouse has reached double-digit temperatures overnight (10°C/50°F), usually in late spring, the chillies are transitioned to the greenhouse, where they remain for the rest of the growing season.

In contrast to this, faster-growing climbing beans are also tender plants that will succumb to frost and require warm temperatures to germinate. However, they establish quickly outside once all risk of frost has passed. So I tend to wait until the beginning of June, then sow these direct into a raised bed outside in the kitchen garden.

TOP LEFT *Chillies sown early February under grow lights.*
TOP RIGHT *Newly emerged garlic sown the previous autumn.*
BOTTOM LEFT *Summer squash seeds germinating at the beginning of April.*
BOTTOM RIGHT *January-sown sweet peas putting on side shoots in the greenhouse.*

Both flower and vegetable seeds can be started off in a number of ways. After a while you'll find a process that works for you, so your house is not overcrowded with seedlings all started off at the same time! There are a few steps I follow without fail each spring to make sure I give everything the best possible beginning.

Washing pots This is particularly important to prevent fungal diseases such as damping off, which can infect seedlings, weakening and killing them. I rinse or tap out the pots and remove any remaining soil, then clean them thoroughly with hot soapy water and a pot scrubber, before leaving outside to dry.

Cleaning plant labels For plastic labels I use a cotton pad with a dab of nail polish remover to remove marker pen. For wooden labels, a piece of medium to fine sandpaper will remove last year's writing.

Compost There is a lot available on the market in terms of seed-starting mixes and potting-on composts, along with different mixes for different stages of the growing cycle. When I first began gardening, I found this quite overwhelming. However, as I gained more growing experience I realized a peat-free, multi-purpose compost is suitable for almost all seeds. If a seedling requires good drainage I will add a handful of horticultural grit to the mix. Where moisture is key, topping the tray with a fine sprinkling of vermiculite once I've sown the seeds is very effective.

Sowing seeds This is in most cases as easy as following the directions on the seed packet. (If the seed packet is lacking instructions, a quick search online will provide the necessary information.) Pre-moistening compost until it just holds together has become standard practice. It prevents air pockets (which plant roots do not like) and makes it easier to fill pots or trays quickly.

Comforting Cauliflower Soup

My eldest daughter Mia, or Mimi as I call her, is without a doubt the best cook in our house. This is one of her recipes and it's a crowd pleaser. A delicious soup recipe for those spring days that still beg to be called winter.

Serves 4

1 medium cauliflower
2 tbsp olive oil, plus extra for drizzling
Salt, to taste
A knob of butter
1 onion (red or white), chopped
1 clove garlic, finely chopped
½ tsp grated nutmeg
960ml (1¾ pints) vegetable stock
A squeeze of lemon juice

Preheat the oven to 220°C/200°C fan/425°F/gas mark 7.

Chop the cauliflower into small pieces and lay out on a tray, then drizzle with olive oil and scatter over a pinch of salt. Roast in the oven for 15 minutes until golden brown.

Meanwhile, heat the 2 tablespoons of olive oil and butter in a heavy-based saucepan over a medium heat. Add the onions and garlic and cook until soft and translucent. Add the nutmeg and stir for 5 minutes until fragrant. Next add the vegetable stock and cook for a further 5 minutes.

Remove the cauliflower from the oven and add it to the broth. Let it simmer for 15 minutes, stirring occasionally. Remove from the heat and allow to cool down a little before blending until smooth. Add a squeeze of lemon and salt to taste.

Serve with buttered soda bread or sourdough.

Caper Linguine
with Crispy Purple Sprouting Broccoli

Whether Mimi's following a recipe or making it up as she goes, we are all very thankful to sit down to one of her taste sensations. Her caper sauce was one of those instant hits. A quick and easy dish on paper that Mimi threw together one evening, which offers a lovely depth of flavour in such a short amount of time.

Serves 4

140g (5oz) purple sprouting broccoli
Salt, to taste
2 tbsp olive oil, plus extra for drizzling
300g (10oz) your favourite pasta
2 tbsp unsalted butter plus an extra knob
6 garlic cloves, finely chopped
2 heaped tbsp capers
240ml (8fl oz) white wine
2 tbsp freshly squeezed lemon juice
45g (1½oz) grated Parmesan

Preheat the oven to 180°C/160°C fan/350°F/gas mark 4.

Lay the broccoli on a baking sheet lined with baking paper, then sprinkle with salt and drizzle with olive oil. Mix until all the stems are coated then lay them out flat. Bake for 15 minutes or until the edges are crispy and slightly browned.

Meanwhile, bring a pot of water to the boil with a pinch of salt, add the pasta and simmer according to the packet instructions or until cooked al dente. Drain and set to one side.

In a heavy-based pan on a medium heat, add the 2 tablespoons of oil and melt in the butter. Reduce the heat slightly and add the garlic and capers to the pan. Cook until very soft but don't allow them to brown. Add the wine and a knob of butter and stir occasionally until the wine has reduced. Add a good squeeze of lemon juice and half the Parmesan.

Toss the pasta into the pan and stir until well combined. Serve immediately with the remaining Parmesan and the broccoli on the side.

Peas in guttering

I discovered this method for sowing peas through an online growing community towards the beginning of my gardening journey, and it's one that I now return to year after year. It is not only a great greenhouse spacesaver, but it also stops rodents reaching your delicious pea seeds for a nibble. This is also a very useful technique for growing early crops of microgreens and lettuces. All you need to do is simply clip the guttering section to an internal potting shed wall or greenhouse frame. However, if you are doing this inside a potting shed, make sure there is plenty of natural daylight.

YOU WILL NEED
- A length of old guttering
- A drill or sharp implement to create drainage holes
- Clip-on brackets (found in hardware stores)
- Pea seeds
- Peat-free multi-purpose compost
- Vermiculite for topping (optional)

METHOD

Make

Carefully drill holes along a length of guttering about every 10cm (4 inches), before attaching it with brackets to the internal supports of a greenhouse frame.

Sow

An optional step is to soak the pea seeds in a bowl of water for 8–12 hours or a maximum of 24 hours prior to sowing, in order to soften the hard outer layer and allow the shoot to push through more easily. It is not essential, but it works well for me.

Fill the guttering with compost, then sow the pea seeds along its length, a few centimetres apart and a centimetre deep. Topping with a layer of vermiculite will prevent the soil drying out too quickly. Keep the soil moist at all times after sowing. Once your seedlings are around 5–7.5cm (2–3 inches) tall, start to harden them off so they are ready to go outside (see page 83).

Plant out

To plant out, dig a trench the depth, length and slightly wider than the guttering in a raised bed or border. Carefully remove the guttering from the brackets and water the seedlings, as this makes it easier to slide them out and into the trench. Place one end of the guttering into the trench, using a trowel to loosen the plants from the sides of the guttering, then gently slide them out into the soil. Firm around each plant, and give them another quick water to settle the soil. Don't forget to provide supports for your peas to climb up.

Spring garden tasks

Plants are less likely to suffer shock, disease or scorch if they are planted or pruned on a mild dry day, which is why the majority of plant disturbance – planting, pruning, dividing and propagating – is undertaken in spring or autumn, when the weather is at its most temperate. Hopefully! Before tackling any such jobs, check the forecast. You are looking for a couple of dry days back to back with no extreme spikes or dips in temperature.

Here are a few of the most pressing jobs you'll need to do in your garden in spring or autumn.

1. Border clean up

Pull out any remaining annuals in spring if you haven't done so over winter and remove any dead foliage from around perennials. If you look closely around the base of the plants you may see new spring growth start to emerge. Any disease-free foliage that you have removed can be placed on the compost pile.

2. Dividing

Use a clean spade or two garden forks to 'divide' established perennials and create free plants. Simply dig up a plant that is getting too big for its space, and gently lift it out of the ground. Remove any loose dirt around the rootball so you can clearly see the roots, then pull apart the rootball into sections – depending on the size and type of plant, a firm slice with a clean and sharp spade might be enough to separate the roots, or you might need to place two garden forks back to back and push them apart to divide the roots. For really woody plants, you might find yourself resorting to a saw! Perennials are tough and will usually not bat an eyelid at what seems like brutal treatment. Do check the specifics of each plant before you go ahead; lupins, for example, have a long central tap root and success in creating new plants is more likely from cuttings rather than division.

continues...

3. Cuttings

The basic process for most softwood plants is snipping off a few centimetres of active growth, removing all but a couple of leaves from the stem and potting up in a gritty compost. Water in well and cover with a propagator lid and in a few weeks you should see active growth. Dipping the stem into a rooting powder will help to encourage new root growth quickly. Cuttings can be taken from spring through to autumn. Softwood cuttings tend to be more successful if tackled from spring to early summer; hardwood cuttings are best taken in autumn.

4. Transplanting

Spring is the perfect time to move plants around if they are not thriving in a particular spot or you're just not happy with their placement. Make sure to dig up a good-size rootball along with the plant to prevent shocking it.

5. Pruning

Spring-blooming perennial shrubs, such as forsythia, lily of the valley and lilacs, flower on last year's growth (old wood). In order for them to flower again the following spring, they have to be pruned immediately after flowering to allow the shrub enough time throughout the season to grow the stems for next year's flowers. By contrast, summer bloomers such as *Hydrangea paniculata* and roses will flower on the current year's growth (new wood). If you're unsure, remember this handy rhyme:

> *If it blooms before June do not spring prune,*
> *wait until immediately after it's bloomed.*

When pruning any perennial, remove diseased, damaged or dead stems first. Aiming for good airflow around the plant and a pleasing shape will keep it happy and reduce the risk of disease. Always use clean pruners, and clean them between cutting each plant. For woody stems over 1cm (½ inch) in thickness, use anvil pruners rather than bypass secateurs for sharp, clean cuts, as crushed stems may introduce disease.

*Naturalized bluebells on two levels creating an unexpected
tiered effect and giving much-needed early spring colour.*

Potatoes in containers

Growing in containers is an excellent spacesaver for smaller gardens. Beyond that, container growing in general is also very useful for areas with a shorter growing season, as you can start off your half-hardy and tender crops earlier than usual within a greenhouse, polytunnel or cold frame, then move them outside once the risk of frost has passed. I also like this method because undoubtedly when harvesting potatoes from a bed, one or two will be missed no matter how much time you spend sifting through the soil. Growing this way is also useful at harvest time, because containers can be pulled back into the greenhouse late in the growing season and the potatoes cropped as needed rather than having to be lifted all at once.

YOU WILL NEED
- **Seed potatoes of your choice** Charlotte, Rocket and International Kidney are my favourites of the earlier varieties. Sarpo Mira is a lovely all-round potato for mashing, roasting and chips, plus it is very blight resistant.
- **Containers** Purpose-made grow bags, galvanized steel tubs and repurposed plastic containers are all good for potato growing. Anywhere from 30–40 litres in capacity is good, size wise.
- **Peat-free multi-purpose compost** Potatoes are heavy feeders, so adding organic matter to the compost will provide an extra boost of nutrients to help them to form larger tubers.

METHOD
Plant
Fill your container a third of the way with the enriched compost. Place two (maincrop variety) or three (early variety) seed potatoes into the soil with the eyes (the little sprouts on the potatoes) facing upwards. Cover with another few centimetres of compost and water them in. Once the foliage has reached 7.5–12cm (3–5 inches) above the soil, top with fresh compost to create a mound of soil around the seed potato (known as 'earthing up'). As the foliage emerges, repeat this process until the soil reaches the top of the bag.

Harvest
Early potatoes are ready once the plant has begun to flower. Maincrop varieties are ready once the foliage has browned. If you don't plan to lift maincrop varieties straightaway, cut away the dead foliage and leave the potatoes in the compost until needed.

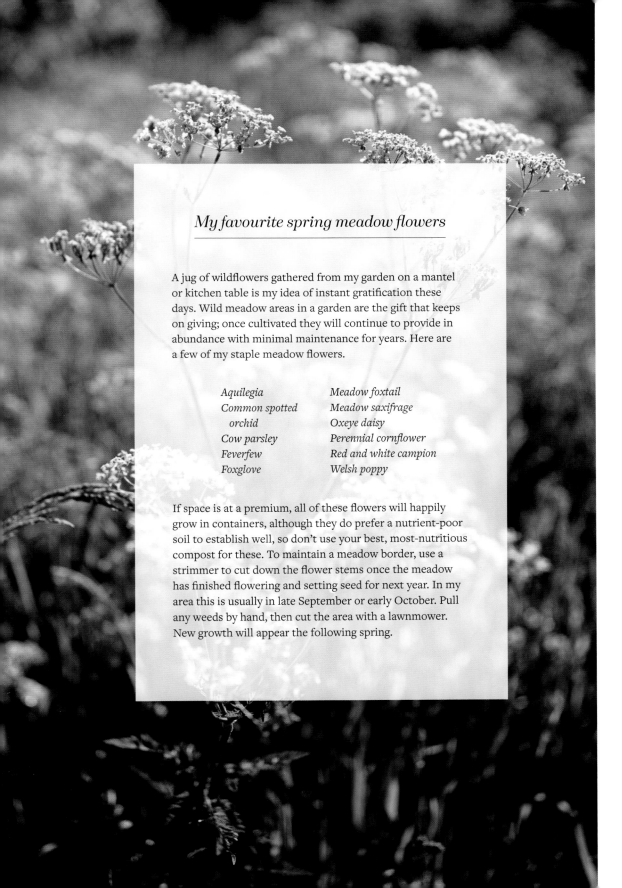

My favourite spring meadow flowers

A jug of wildflowers gathered from my garden on a mantel or kitchen table is my idea of instant gratification these days. Wild meadow areas in a garden are the gift that keeps on giving; once cultivated they will continue to provide in abundance with minimal maintenance for years. Here are a few of my staple meadow flowers.

Aquilegia	*Meadow foxtail*
Common spotted	*Meadow saxifrage*
orchid	*Oxeye daisy*
Cow parsley	*Perennial cornflower*
Feverfew	*Red and white campion*
Foxglove	*Welsh poppy*

If space is at a premium, all of these flowers will happily grow in containers, although they do prefer a nutrient-poor soil to establish well, so don't use your best, most-nutritious compost for these. To maintain a meadow border, use a strimmer to cut down the flower stems once the meadow has finished flowering and setting seed for next year. In my area this is usually in late September or early October. Pull any weeds by hand, then cut the area with a lawnmower. New growth will appear the following spring.

Compost

Homemade compost may just be the gold standard of composts for your vegetable and flower crops, with literally zero carbon footprint or cost. The soil will thank you for it, rewarding you with bountiful crops and flowers. To produce the best compost, your pile will need a mix of both carbon- and nitrogen-rich organic waste. To make a mix that maintains a good level of oxygen, add two buckets of carbon-rich matter to one bucket of nitrogen-rich matter.

Carbon-rich or brown waste	**Nitrogen-rich or green waste**
Wood ash	Grass clippings
Coffee grounds	Fruit and vegetable scraps
Cardboard	Tea leaves
Straw	Seaweed
Paper / newspaper	Comfrey leaves
Dried leaves	Chicken manure
Eggshells	Flower cuttings
Twigs and branches	

It's a common myth that compost piles give off bad odours, as this is only true if the pile is holding too much water or has an imbalance of materials – usually too little carbon. When creating compost bays, two to three sections is ideal – if space is unlimited – so you can turn over the compost frequently to release further oxygen. This will prevent the pile becoming stagnant. An old dustbin with 2.5cm (1 inch) holes drilled around the outside for good airflow also makes a good compost solution. Purpose-built sealed units are good for gardens where rodents are already present. The compost is ready when it is dark brown, crumbly in texture and has no odour.

Here are a few tips for getting the best out of your compost pile.

1. Add brown and green waste in layers to avoid clumps of either (see left).
2. Before adding leaves, shred them, and chop up twigs and branches as much as possible to speed up the decomposition process.
3. In particularly dry spells, keep the compost pile moist.
4. Completely turn over the compost pile every 3–6 weeks to keep the temperature and oxygen levels high.
5. In extreme weather, high heat or an extended period of rain, cover the compost bay to keep moisture levels stable.
6. Diseased plants and weeds should not be added to a compost pile, but disposed of separately, or else they may spread throughout the compost.

Summer

Simply summertime

The transitional days from winter to spring and summer to autumn are visually the most inspiring to me. Trying to spot the very first subtle changes that signal the arrival of a new season brings a quiet feeling of rejuvenation and mentally kick-starts my motivation for fresh projects, both indoors and out. Summer, however, is the season when I slow down – or at least try to – to observe and relish the completed projects of seasons past as well as a garden in lush, fresh bloom.

You'll often find me outside with the sunrise, still in my PJs and whatever shoes are lying closest to the bootroom door, with the first cuppa of the day in hand. In the early morning quiet I wander from bed to bed looking for new blooms, and note the progress on everything from roses to tomatoes. I'll take the opportunity to water the kitchen garden early if a hot day is on the horizon, and snack on some fresh peas that I pick while opening the greenhouse.

Early morning is the best time to gather produce from the kitchen garden and also flowers from the potager – they are less likely to wilt and will remain at their freshest for longer. Having a bucket of water to pop the blooms into, along with a sharp pair of snips, makes this an easy task.

As I go along, I make mental notes, or if I'm really prepared I pull up a notes app on my phone and jot down future planting ideas and dividing or transplanting tasks for the early autumn months or following spring.

By now the kitchen garden has started to produce the first early crops. They are often very small, and never enough for a meal, so they hardly ever make it to the kitchen – but, my word, how rewarding they are; a single strawberry, the first peppery radish, a handful of spinach. Garden joy...

With any luck, by the beginning of June the final frosts have passed and I can get stuck into planting out tender annual vegetables and flowers, emptying my jam-packed greenhouse to make way for too many tomato plants and a myriad of chillies. (I recommend checking your local weather forecast regularly if frosts in June are something you have to deal with.)

As spring fades, we enter what is undoubtedly one of the most satisfying times in the growing season.

The summer
garden

Hardening off and planting out

As the expected last frost date approaches, there is a sense of anticipation in the air. The greenhouse is bursting at the seams with lovingly nurtured seedlings ready to break free from their containers and explode with new growth once they reach the fertile ground outdoors. It's the time of year where you'll find me checking the weather app on my phone sometimes twice daily, scanning for highly unwelcome cold spells.

As a rule of thumb, I aim to harden off seedlings for a good 7–10 days before planting out. In my first year of growing, the temperature went from cool spring to a high-summer heatwave overnight. So, I made the risky decision to plant everything out without hardening off after checking the 10-day forecast was calling for more of the same almost tropical temps. Weighing it up, the plants were better off outside in the ground than melting in the greenhouse. Thankfully, they made the transition without batting an eyelid, and quickly settled into their new homes.

However, if not hardened off correctly, most seedlings can suffer from cold shock or wind burn, and although most will recover over time, growth is likely to be stunted or set back as a result. To avoid this, I follow these steps, which apply to both tender vegetable and flower seedlings.

1. The process of toughening up seedlings for their new life outside should, most important of all, be a gradual one. Put them outside for 1–2 hours a day, then work up to a full day and night outdoors by day 10.

2. For the first few days, place your plants in a location outdoors that is protected from the worst of the wind. This is when a cold frame is nice to have, as you can just lift the lid to expose plants to outside temperatures before lowering it again to protect them without the need to haul plants in and out of the greenhouse. After five years of growing at Greenfields, I still haven't got round to building myself one – perhaps this will be the year!

3. Once hardened off and planted out into their final positions, keep some horticultural fleece or cloches handy to cover seedlings should any unexpected frosty weather crop up on the forecast.

Pumpkins

Growing pumpkins and winter squashes in general has surged in popularity in recent years. With so many weird and wonderful varieties to try, along with their many uses from culinary (see recipe on page 148) to decorative (see page 139), they have become a must-grow in my garden. Some of my favourites are 'Cinderella', 'Crown Prince', 'Turk's Turban', 'Baby Boo' and 'Jill Be Little'. The last two are good options for smaller gardens.

1. Sow

In my area, pumpkins do best when started off from seed indoors in spring. I sow one seed per 9cm (3½ inch) pot in moistened, peat-free compost. A good tip is to sow the seed on its side to prevent rotting. Pumpkins do not benefit from an early sowing; around 4–6 weeks before your last frost date is early enough and will produce a good-size seedling.

2. Harden off

Plant out your pumpkins not just after the last frost, but when the day's warmth is beginning to stretch well into the evening. I like to wait until my weather app is showing at least double digits at night before making the leap. Pumpkins are a tender annual, they do not like cold and will not survive a frost. If they become stunted early on in their growth, due to harsh winds or a sudden drop in temperature, they may not recover enough to produce a healthy crop.

Harden off your potted pumpkins by gradually introducing them to the outdoors. I start them off for an hour a day in a spot protected from direct wind, then increase the length of time they are out there gradually over a week until they are able to fend for themselves overnight. (See page 83 for more on hardening off.)

3. Plant

Dig a planting hole that's at least 30cm (12 inches) wide. Generously mix in some well-rotted horse or chicken manure, peat-free shop-bought compost or, even better, homemade compost. Do be generous, as all types of squash are heavy feeders. Add more organic material to the soil that you dug out from your planting hole and use this mix to backfill around the plant.

Make sure you leave a generous distance between each plant. I aim for 2 metres (6½ feet) between my winter squash so they may sprawl out along the ground. Summer squashes don't take up as much space; 1 metre (3 feet) square is usually enough room for a courgette plant to spread out.

4. Grow vertically

If you would like to train your vine crops to grow vertically – a great space-saving idea for smaller gardens – do so over an existing structure like an arbour or obelisk, or build your own trellis or teepee from hazel sticks or another variety of strong, fairly straight lengths of wood. Bamboo canes also work well for smaller squash varieties. As the fruit sets on the vine they bulk up in weight quickly and may easily snap off a weaker stem. Support the fruit from underneath by resting them in a hammock made from an old pair of tights to take the weight, securing the ends to the nearest overhead support.

5. Feed

Once planted, firm the soil well with your hands and water in. I like to push soil around the plant to create a barrier for the squash. This helps to keep the water in, especially if gardening on a slope. All varieties need lots of water and do not like to dry out, so you can expect to give them a good drink every couple of days during hot dry spells. As soon as the first fruits appear, feed them fortnightly with a liquid seaweed or tomato feed, watering around the base of the plant, not the leaves.

Nasturtium 'Purple Emperor' trained up bamboo teepees, cornflowers, dwarf sunflowers, pumpkins and winter squash soaking up the late August sunshine.

Pumpkin growing tips

1

Plant your pumpkins close to pollinator-attracting flowers. Nasturtiums, sunflowers and lavender in particular are pollinator magnets, which your pumpkins will need in spades in order to set fruit. If your garden, like mine, is rather exposed to the elements, and often fairly wet, replace lavender with nepeta (catmint), which can handle a lot more water and attracts bees and butterflies en masse.

2

Around 4–6 weeks before your first expected frost, remove any new flower buds and any immature fruits, as these will likely not size up or ripen in time. This allows the plant's energy to focus solely on ripening the larger fruits. Nip off any larger leaves casting shade to allow the sunshine in.

3

Place burgeoning pumpkins on flat rocks or in a cushion of straw to prevent them rotting on the soil. Beware, though, as slugs love the dark, slightly moist habitat underneath pumpkins. A careful check every once in a while to rehouse them is in your pumpkins' best interests!

4

If an early frost is expected, snip the fruits off the main vine, leaving as much stem as possible – at least 7.5cm (3 inches) helps to prevent premature rotting. Gently place them somewhere warm and dry, with good light and airflow, to allow your pumpkins time for the skin to harden thoroughly – the harder the skin, the longer they will store. Cured pumpkins will last up to three months in cool, dry conditions at a temperature of around 10°C (50°F).

Summer in the kitchen garden

The trough is planted up with a mixture of sunflowers and snapdragons. New potatoes in grow bags are lined up between the beds. Courgettes and small winter squashes are dotted around in pots. The first calendula flowers provide a hint of high summer colour still to come, among autumn-planted garlic standing tall like giant blades of grass.

Garden entertaining

My motto for summer entertaining is seasonal, simple and welcoming. We dine al fresco as much as the Scottish weather will allow, on recipes thought up that morning from what is ready for picking. The table will be scattered with bud vases filled with a flower or two from the cutting garden. Drinks will include mojitos with crushed mint, *gin and tonics with a sprig of rosemary and pitchers of mint water.*

To make mint water: *Steep a handful of mint leaves in boiling water for 10–15 minutes. Leave to cool before pouring into a jug or pitcher. Add 7 cups of ice-cold water and a few ice cubes before serving.*

Kitchen garden care

Crops that don't have to compete with weeds and have a continual supply of nutrients will produce stronger plants and in turn larger yields. That said, here are some jobs to tackle throughout the growing season.

1. In raised beds or in the ground
- Keep on top of weeds. As I settled into the rhythm of gardening and a slower pace in general, my view of weeding changed drastically. It's almost meditative now, allowing time to clear the mind as well as the weeds!
- Check and tie in climbing vines weekly to prevent stems snapping as they grow.
Earth up the soil around potatoes to prevent light reaching the forming tubers, turning them green and inedible.
- Pick pea and bean crops regularly to encourage further fruiting.
- Mulch with straw, or place a piece of cardboard or tile underneath, forming and ripening fruits such as squashes and strawberries, to prevent them from rotting.

2. In the greenhouse
- Feed crops such as chillies, tomatoes, cucumbers and aubergines weekly once fruit has set, using a high-potash feed such as a tomato or liquid seaweed feed. Fruit sets after the flowers die and the fruit begins to emerge.
- Snip off side shoots regularly on vining tomato varieties, to focus the plant's energy on producing fruit rather than foliage. A side shoot is a small stem that grows between the vertical main stem and a main side branch, at roughly a 45-degree angle.

3. Watering
Watering early in the day prevents plants scorching in the midday sun and uses less water. To prevent scorching further, aim the water around the base of the plants rather than onto the leaves.

4. Tools
Clean pruners, shears and other tools regularly throughout the season to prevent the spread of pests and diseases from plant to plant.

My favourite
perennial flowers for cutting

Allium

A hardy, bulbous perennial in so many shapes and forms. Display as a bunch on their own or use single stems to add drama to an arrangement. They are worth their weight in the garden.

Astrantia major

A hardy perennial requiring little maintenance. The deep, lush claret of Astrantia 'Roma' adds depth to any arrangement.

Cow parsley

Not to be mistaken with the very similar hemlock, which is poisonous. Cow parsley can add much-needed froth to an arrangement.

Forsythia

With a flowering time from February to April, a few forsythia branches can be the perfect addition to a spring arrangement or wreath.

Hellebores

The double varieties, especially in dusky pinks and buttery yellows, are my favourites and look positively spring-like in a generous bunch on the kitchen table.

Lupins

A hardy perennial. I love lupins for their upright structure and the little flower puffs that cover the stems.

Nepeta

What a statement this hardy perennial makes on its own in a vase! It has a long vase life and the vibrant purple blooms really make an impact.

Roses

Where would we be without them?

A pollinator's paradise

Discovering ways to encourage a lively insect and bird population back to the garden has been a journey of great reward. Bees have returned in droves, along with butterflies, moths, hedgehogs, dragonflies, frogs and, my favourite of all, ladybirds. Each has an important role to play in the garden, from pollination to pest control.

As well as caring for our pollinator friends such as bees and butterflies, there are many other insects to encourage to the garden. Lacewings, parasitic wasps and ground beetles, among others, play an important role in providing balance, as well as natural pest control. Earwigs, often seen as a friend and foe, are great for keeping blackfly under control – but love to eat dahlia blooms if they discover them. Rather than trying to keep them out, round them up from dark crevices at dusk before rehousing to a blackfly problem area. (For more tips on insect-friendly pest control, see page 108.)

Here are a few ways to create a pollinator's paradise.

• Leave a section of grass to grow unchecked all summer long to encourage myriad bugs, beetles, moths and birds.

• Sow a wildflower meadow. There are meadow mixes available to purchase to suit all types of soil and location, from full sun to part shade, including annual and perennial mixes. Even one square metre of wildflowers can make a hugely positive impact on insect biodiversity in the garden.

• Make a wildlife pond or trough to encourage frogs, dragonflies and newts. In time, the frogs will keep slugs and snails to a minimum.

• Fix bird or owl boxes to mature trees in autumn or winter to encourage new nesters the following spring.

• Place bird feeders around the garden along with a bird bath. Between refills, wash bird feeders with a scrubbing brush using a mild soap and hot water solution to prevent the spread of bacteria.

• Bug hotels are another easy habitat to DIY, which will welcome solitary bees and bugs to the garden.

• Give your pollinators a feast rich in pollen and nectar by including the following flowers in your garden: sunflowers, dahlias (in particular those with nectar-rich single flowers), marigolds, lavender, nepeta, borage and snapdragons.

Dahlias

Dahlias are the jewel of late summer in my garden. With literally thousands of cultivars available, the only difficulty you'll have with these delightful flowers is choosing which varieties to grow. Between the Pompoms, Cactus, Collarette and Decorative (just to name a few) types, there is something for everyone, including those that work well in containers, should space be limited. My favourites over the last couple of years are the singles, which have the most open centres that allow pollinators to feast. They are fairly easy to grow and maintain, and absolutely worth the effort required.

Here is a seasonal step-by-step care guide to create a dazzling dahlia display.

Spring

Pot up any tubers that have overwintered out of the ground (see Autumn, over the page) into pots of good-quality, peat-free, multi-purpose compost about 4–5 weeks before your average last frost date. Aim to plant in a pot that gives a snug, but not tight, fit, to reduce the amount of compost needed. Water them in and keep them in a frost-free location – a greenhouse or shed is perfect.

When the first shoots appear, make sure they are receiving ample amounts of light, to prevent weak, leggy stems. Harden off gradually (see page 83) and plant them out at least 30–46cm (12–18 inches) apart and roughly 10–15cm (4–6 inches) deep. I aim to plant out once the risk of frosts are long gone and the nights are balmy. Staking taller varieties is worthwhile at this stage, while the plants are small and easy to work around. Bamboo canes, hazel branches, or metal circular supports are all great choices.

Dahlias need a full-sun location, with shelter from the worst of the wind. Good drainage is also key to a happy plant. Adding a sprinkle of mycorrhizal fungi (which can be bought from garden centres or online) to the planting hole, along with well-rotted manure or a good compost, will help your dahlias establish quickly.

Summer

Keep on top of watering in dry spells. Feed once every two weeks with a seaweed or tomato feed and deadhead to promote more flowers.

SUMMER

99

TIP

Not sure which buds are new and which are spent? Spent blooms are conical, with a pointy tip; new buds are rounder with a flatter top.

Autumn

Dahlia season comes to an abrupt end once the first hard frost appears, quickly blackening the plant and stopping any new blooms in their tracks.

In warmer climates, dahlias can be left in the ground to overwinter. Just cut the stems back to ground level once blackened by the first frosts, mulch them well, and they will happily fall into dormancy to return the following spring. However, if you live in a colder climate, like me, where negative Celsius temperatures are a common feature over the winter months, you may need to lift and store your dahlia tubers.

Once blackened by the frost, use a fork to carefully lift the tubers from the ground. Rinse off the excess soil and leave them to dry in the greenhouse or shed for a few days. To store, I wrap the tubers individually in newspaper, fish-and-chip-shop style, with a sprinkling of vermiculite to soak up any remaining moisture before storing them in the shed.

Winter

Once a month, check your dahlias are storing well. If there is too much moisture in the air they may rot, so a well-ventilated, frost-free location is essential.

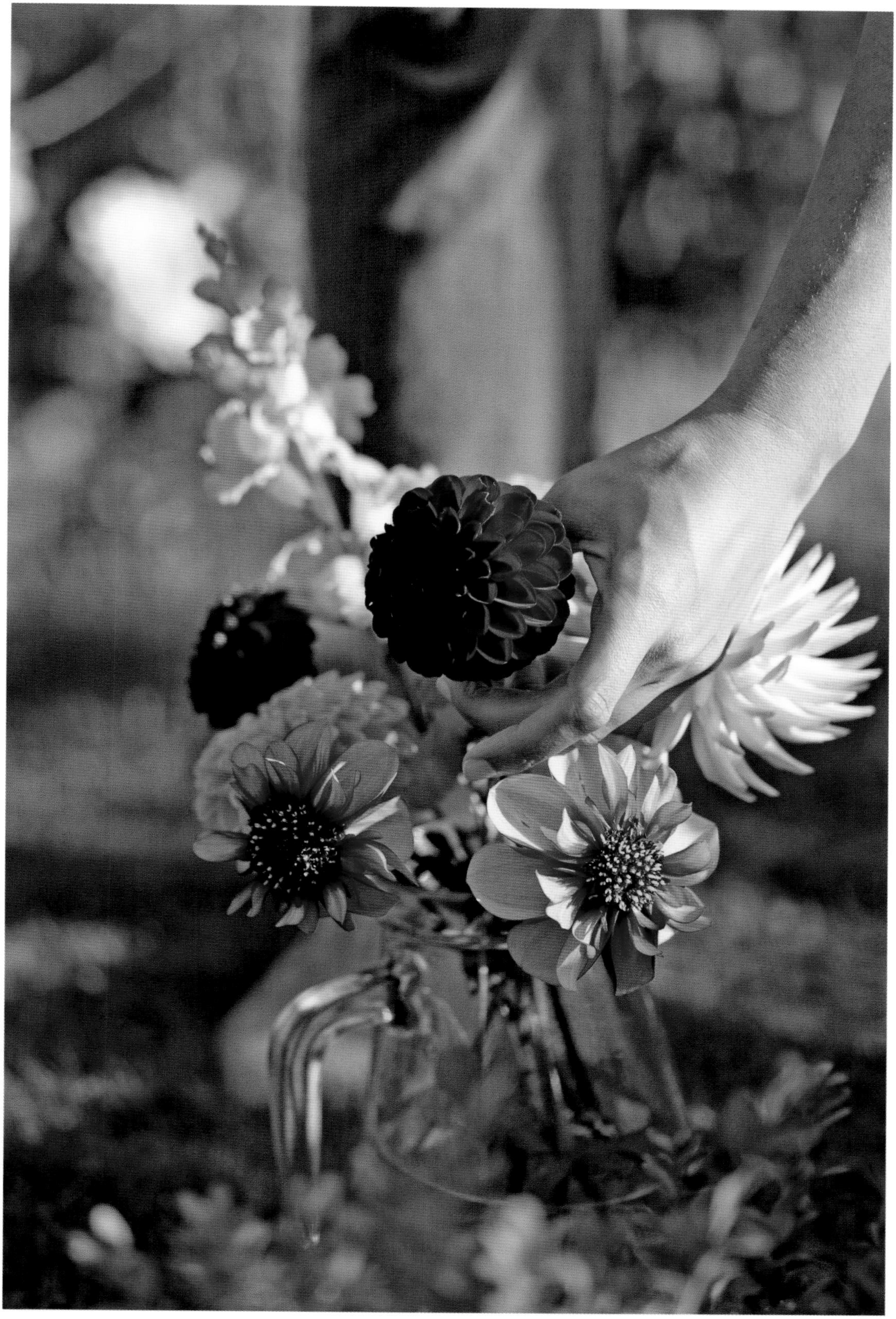

The growth cycle

The ability to grow organically and sustainably is a gift to us all. If done well, the process of growing can create the ultimate circular economy; seeds can be saved from almost all crops for replanting the following year, while spent plant matter can be added to the compost heap to add nutrients back into the soil for the next growing season. Thus zero waste and zero-carbon miles create organic home-grown produce that just tastes better!

Harvesting, curing and storing

The summer months can produce a bumper, rainbow array of crops that you can't always eat fast enough to avoid waste. So here's my guide to harvesting, curing and storing my favourite kitchen garden crops and ensuring as little wastage as possible.

Crop	Harvest	Cure	Store	Storage life
Beans (broad)	Snip the pod from the plant	Not needed	Rinse and shell, blanch in boiling water for 3 minutes, store in an airtight container in the freezer	12 months
Beans (borlotti)	Pick once the pods are beginning to dry and shrivel up	Shell the beans and dry further in a single layer on a tray	Store in an airtight container	12 months
Garlic	Harvest once the tips of the plant and the lower leaves are starting to brown. Lift using a fork or trowel	Hang in twine-tied bunches of 5–8 bulbs or lay on a drying rack in a cool, dry, well-ventilated location for 14–21 days	Braid the garlic or remove the stem and roots and store in a wire basket in a cool, dry location	9 months
Potatoes (maincrop)	Dig up carefully with a fork once the plant has started to die back	Dry in a single layer, in a dark, cold, well-ventilated location such as a shed until the skin is fully formed and dry	Store in hessian sacks in a dark, cool and dry location	6–9 months
Onions Shallots	Harvest once the stems have flopped over and are starting to brown	Dry in a single layer in the greenhouse for 10–14 days until the skin and stems are fully dried	Remove the stem and store in a wire basket in a cool, dry location	6 months
Chillies	Harvest once ripe according to the variety	Thread string through each stem and hang up or lay flat to cure until shrivelled	Store hanging or in a wire basket in a cool, dry location	6 months
Carrots Parsnips	Harvest as needed, leaving the rest in the ground. Frosts will enhance the sugars in these root vegetables, making them sweeter			
Tomatoes	Any tomatoes left at the end of the growing season – ripe or unripe – can be preserved in a green tomato chutney (see recipe on page 150)			

Summer garden tasks

Here are some tips that work for me to keep the summer garden looking and performing well all season long.

1. Zone your garden maintenance
Split your garden areas into zones and assign each to a day of the week. As an example, on Mondays I only look at the plant theatre in terms of maintenance. On that day I will weed, fertilize, deadhead and check for any pest issues. Once I've finished, I won't work on this spot again until the following Monday. This process really works to help break up garden tasks and prevents the garden from getting out of control and becoming overwhelming.

2. Watering
Watering in the early morning or early evening really allows plants to absorb as much water as possible before the heat of the day sets in. Watering with rainwater is better for the garden as the pH level is closer to that of the plants and soil, plus it saves tap water so is better for the environment and your wallet. If you don't have one already, consider installing a water butt to collect rainwater from guttering.

3. Seed-starting trays and pots
If you use reusable containers to start off your seeds in spring, summer is an excellent time to clean all of your supplies now you've planted out their inhabitants. Wash them thoroughly using hot soapy water, rinse well and lay them out in the sun to dry. Once dry, store them somewhere under cover so they are ready to use for autumn or next spring's sowing projects. This task not only gets you ahead and ready for later sowing, but it is also much more pleasant to tackle on a warm summer's day than a cold winter one!

4. Deadheading
Keep nipping off spent blooms on flowers such as cosmos, cornflowers, roses, dahlias, lupins and calendula to promote more flowers all summer long.

Common garden pests and how to treat them naturally

In a new growing space, you'll often find your well-cared-for vegetables and fruit are left alone for the first year, your brassicas are pristine without a caterpillar nibble in sight, and slugs... what slugs? This was true for my kitchen garden, but by the second year of growing, everyone knew where the growing party was at, so it was time to protect them or lose them.

TIP

Hostas are often plagued by slugs and snails. Try planting them in pots near a bird feeder. Song thrushes in particular love to snack on slugs and snails, which will help keep your hosta leaves intact.

Problem	What they love	How to stop them in their tracks
Aphids (blackfly/greenfly) can be found in clusters sticking like glue underneath the leaves and along the stems of affected plants	Most plants, apart from those of the pungent variety, such as alliums and herbs	Plant a sacrificial crop, such as marigolds, near tomatoes to deter the aphids. Encourage birds, ladybirds and lacewings to the garden and they will happily keep the aphid population under control for you. The odd spider in the greenhouse will do wonders for keeping unwanted critters at bay
Cabbage white butterfly (a pretty white butterfly), causes mass destruction, laying eggs on your crops that will grow into hungry caterpillars that will munch through the lot	Brassicas	Mesh the brassicas as you plant them out using a fine mesh that's staked tautly around the plants. Be sure not to leave any gaps, as they will be discovered
Slugs and snails	Strawberries, lupins, courgettes, beans, lettuces, brassicas and cucumbers, parsley, dahlias, hostas, delphiniums and dill – to name a few of their favourite snacks	There are lots of options to experiment with: crushed eggshells around the base of plants works particularly well in my garden. Best found and rehoused at dusk or early evening with the help of a torch. Look under pots and in the corners of raised beds. Create a haven for frogs and birds and they will happily feast on slugs and snails
Grey squirrels	Bulbs, particularly tulips and crocuses	After planting, cover bulbs with chicken wire until the shoots appear in spring. If planting in containers, add a top layer of horticultural grit or gravel to your pots. As well as deterring the squirrels, the gravel will make your pots look smart and help with drainage too!
Wasps	The just-ripened fruits of cherry, apple and pear trees	Securing mesh sleeves over tree branches, although unsightly, is effective at protecting fruit from wasps. Use an organic spray such as peppermint oil to repel wasps
Carrot root fly is something you likely won't see or know about until you find your produce is riddled with tiny holes from these critters come harvest time	Carrots, parsnips, celeriac and celery	Put mesh around the plants with at least a metre-high barrier – as root fly can't fly higher than that. Plant onions or garlic nearby, as the scent will cover that of the plants

Garlic Scape Pesto

My first year growing garlic was a very stressful time indeed. I popped my carefully separated precious cloves into my well-prepared raised bed around mid-September and waited weeks... but nothing sprouted. Not a single one!

Come late February – over five months later! – I thought, that's it, they've rotted, all 80 or so of them. A catastrophic fail! Lo and behold, when I'd all but given up hope I spied the first stubby green shoot popping up from an otherwise 'empty' bed. Ten days later I had a full bed of little green shoots rapidly on the rise. Well, my excitement was palpable. They made it through the first five months, so now only five months to go! (Sigh.) Yes, it's a slow-growing crop and you only know if you've successfully grown a decent-sized bulb once you lift them, so patience is key.

After that I got to experience one rewarding milestone after another in the world of garlic growing. First came what I can only describe as garlic gold. Garlic scapes! Those delectable, immature, flower-bulb stalks that shoot up from hard-neck garlic varieties (one layer of cloves around a hard central stem) around two to three weeks before the garlic bulb is ready to harvest. Well, I read that not only are they edible but delicious to boot! So I looked up a recipe online that led me to garlic scape pesto.

Since discovering the recipe, it's become a midsummer must-have that's loved by one and all in my house. I've tweaked the recipe a touch over time. Fewer pine nuts, a touch more olive oil and I do believe we have a recipe worthy of the sacred family recipe tin – a rather special tin that sits on the shelf above the range, where only recipes with the seal of approval from all make it.

To make this rare and simple summer delight, the first step is to harvest the scapes just after the stalks have curled round on themselves. They can be quite intense in flavour depending on the variety, so if you prefer a more subtle version, blanch the scapes whole in salted boiling water for around 30 seconds before popping them into a bowl with iced water to stop them cooking further. Then continue on with the recipe.

Serves 4 as a main
or 6 as a light
supper

400g (14oz) or 12–18 roughly
chopped garlic scapes – bulb
and all if still immature
100g (3½oz) pine nuts
100g (3½oz) grated Parmesan
100g (3½oz) parsley
1–2 tbsp freshly squeezed
lemon juice
A handful of basil leaves
250ml (8½fl oz) olive oil
Salt and black pepper, to taste
Cooked linguine or other
pasta, to serve

Place the scapes, pine nuts, Parmesan, parsley, lemon juice and all but a few leaves of basil into a blender, adding the olive oil gradually and blending until the consistency is smooth. Season with salt and black pepper to taste.

Stir through cooked fresh linguine and garnish with the remainder of the basil leaves. Enjoy al fresco with great company and your favourite tipple.

Transfer any leftover pesto to a clean jar with a lid and top up with a small layer of olive oil to seal, then store in the fridge for up to a week, or transfer to a freezerproof container and store in the freezer. Chopped fresh scapes popped into freezer bags can also be stored in the freezer to extend their season.

Courgette Cake (or Zucchini Bread)

Prior to moving to Greenfields, my family and I spent a brief stint in Oxford. While there, I became good friends with a wonderful American lady called Joanne and her fun family, who had travelled over from the States for a year-long exchange. Our daughters were in the same class at school, and they would often share snacks at breaktimes, one of which would become a treasured family recipe. They called it zucchini bread – otherwise known as courgette cake.

Fast-forward a few years to my first year growing courgettes, and I read about the inevitable glut I would encounter that promised too many courgettes a day to eat. I didn't believe it – this is Scotland, after all – and with erratic and often short summers, I wasn't expecting a vegetable that originates in Italy to do much in my garden.

Well, 67 courgettes later (from just two plants, I might add!), I was certainly proven wrong. Give them good fertile compost, water and sunshine and they will produce excessive amounts. You have been warned.

Very quickly I was looking up recipes with courgettes as the main ingredient. Up there with my favourites are courgette fritters with a spicy dip, courgetti noodles, and stuffed courgette flowers. Yes, you can eat the flowers too, and they are delicious. That said, my go-to recipe is, you guessed it, zucchini bread. My favourite way to eat this is to cut a chunky slice and enjoy it for breakfast with a mug of tea.

Makes two 450g
(1lb) loaves

3 eggs
400g (14oz) brown sugar
200ml (7fl oz) vegetable oil
2 tsp vanilla extract
500g (1lb 2oz) courgette,
 grated
700g (1lb 10oz) self-raising
 flour
1 tsp bicarbonate of soda
3 tsp ground cinnamon

Preheat the oven to 180°C/160°C fan/350°F/gas mark 4
and grease and line your loaf tins.

In a large mixing bowl or stand mixer, combine the eggs,
sugar, oil and vanilla. Squeeze out the excess water from
the courgettes before adding to the bowl next, if you
prefer a firmer bread.

Gently stir in the flour, bicarbonate of soda and
cinnamon and mix until well combined.

Pour the mixture equally into two loaf tins and bake
for 1 hour. To check they are done, insert a wooden
toothpick or a skewer into the centre of the bread. If it
comes out clean, it's ready. Transfer the tins to a wire
rack and leave to cool in the tins before turning out.

Hats off to you if you can wait until the bread has
cooled before having a bite.

Georgia's Summer Smoothie

This recipe is made on repeat over the summer months when spinach and strawberries are in good supply from the kitchen garden. It's simple, packed with vitamin C and utterly delicious. In my house it tastes best when Georgia makes it!

Serves 2

1 banana, chopped in quarters
150g (5oz) strawberries, chopped in half
45g (1½oz) raw spinach
240ml (8fl oz) fresh orange juice
3–4 ice cubes
60ml (2fl oz) oat milk
1 tbsp organic honey (optional)

Add all the ingredients to a blender and blitz until smooth. For a little more sweetness add a tablespoon of good organic honey.

No-bake Raspberry Cheesecake

For garden gluts of strawberries, cherries or raspberries look no further than this simple no-bake cheesecake. This is an absolute crowd pleaser at family gatherings. The only problem is we never seem to make enough!

Serves 6–8

FOR THE CHEESECAKE
600g (1lb 5oz) digestive biscuits
100g (3½oz) butter, melted
420g (15oz) cream cheese
100g (3½oz) icing sugar
250ml (8½fl oz) double cream
A couple of drops of vanilla extract
FOR THE COULIS AND TOPPING
500g (2 punnets) raspberries
2 tbsp sugar

Put the digestives into a reusable freezer bag and crush them by bashing them with a rolling pin, or blitz them in a food processor. Tip into a mixing bowl with the melted butter, stirring to combine and coat. Evenly line the base of a 20–25cm (8–10 inch) spring-form cake tin with the buttered crumbs. Push them down with the back of a spoon – you're aiming for a medium pressure as the biscuit should not be too compacted. Place in the refrigerator to set overnight.

The next day, in an electric mixer bowl, combine the cream cheese and icing sugar on a slow setting while slowly adding the double cream and vanilla extract. Spread the mixture on top of the set base, cover with a plate, then allow the cheesecake to set in the fridge for another hour.

Once set, top with half of the raspberries. To make the coulis, roughly chop the remaining raspberries and place in a saucepan. Add the sugar and bring to a simmer. Stir until the fruit has become soft and broken down. Pass through a sieve to make a smooth sauce, then pour over the cheesecake once cooled. Set in the fridge for another hour.

Before serving, carefully remove the sides of the cake tin. Enjoy!

Creamy New Potato Salad

My take on a potato salad, which tastes even better with new potatoes straight from the garden.

Serves 4–6 as
 a side

115–230g (4–8oz) mayonnaise
1 tsp Dijon mustard
1 shallot, finely chopped
2 pinches of celery salt
Black pepper
A small bunch of chives, roughly chopped
A heaped tablespoon of capers, roughly chopped
  (optional)
10–12 new potatoes, boiled until soft, cooled and
  quartered
4 eggs, almost hard-boiled, peeled and quartered
  lengthways

In a large bowl, mix the mayonnaise, Dijon mustard, shallot, the celery salt, a crack of black pepper, half of the chopped chives, and the capers (if using), until combined.

Add the potatoes and eggs and gently combine until evenly coated. Taste for seasoning and top with the remaining chives.

Andrew's Bruschetta

Andrew put together this bruschetta recipe when we had a highly unusual basil glut. This method takes a little more effort than some other bruschetta recipes, but believe me the extra time is completely worth it!

Serves 8–10

600g (1lb 5oz) tomatoes –
   whatever you have growing in the garden
8 basil leaves, plus extra to garnish
1 tbsp good-quality balsamic vinegar
2 tbsp olive oil, plus extra for brushing
¼ red onion, finely chopped
2–3 garlic cloves, finely chopped
Salt and pepper, to taste
1 ciabatta loaf, or bread of your choice

Bring a pan of water to the boil. Take a sharp knife and cut a small cross into the top of each tomato. Once your water is boiling, add the tomatoes and blanch for 3 minutes. (No need to blanch cherry tomato varieties.) Using tongs, remove the tomatoes to a colander and rinse under a cold tap.

Once the tomatoes are cool enough to handle, remove and discard the skins – they will come away easily. Cut the tomatoes into quarters, or halves if using cherry tomatoes. Grab a bowl and gently squeeze each of the tomatoes over it to remove the seeds and juice. Discard the seeds and juice. Roughly chop the tomatoes into bite-size pieces. This is a rustic dish so there's no need to be exact.

Roll up the basil leaves like a cigar and finely slice. Put the tomatoes, basil, balsamic vinegar and olive oil in a bowl with the chopped onion and garlic. Combine and season with salt and pepper to taste.

Slice the bread into 2 cm (¾ inch) thick slices. Brush both sides with olive oil. Toast the bread on a griddle pan or under the grill until golden. Once toasted, remove and set on a serving platter and add your tomato mix on top. Finish with a touch of black pepper and basil to garnish.

A
u
t
u
m
n

Autumn abundance

Autumn, the time of year when the mature trees that surround our home in a peaceful green canopy take centre stage to hail the end of nature's peak growing season in a blaze of fiery shades. It's heavenly and magical all at once. Just as I enjoy devouring the newness of spring and the luxuriantly long summer days, I am drawn like a magnet to cool autumnal days that still hold hints of warmth in the breeze. Foraging for arrangements or wreaths at this time of year is always particularly rewarding, when ornamental berries have formed on a wide variety of shrubs from pyracantha to hypericums. You'll find autumn-flowering perennials such as skimmia, sedums and echinacea in full swing; and seedheads have dried on *Scabiosa stellata*, alliums, poppies and honesty flowers.

Sinking into the autumn season feels like an extended hug from an old friend. My mind shifts towards comfort food, cosy corners with comfy chairs, good books and a spot to watch the encore that is autumn as the leaves fall. More importantly, it signals a slowing down of time.

Although slowing down can seem a little trickier when a lot of the same jobs tackled during the business of spring are also relevant in autumn, whether it be transplanting perennials, planting bulbs, weeding, mulching or pruning. Autumn gives us a chance to put a hard-working garden to rest for the dormant season, or if you like get a head start on next year's growing season.

However, being selective about the jobs to handle now versus those that can wait until spring can relieve any sense of being overwhelmed. It is also far better for nature's foragers – birds, hedgehogs, squirrels and the like – if the garden isn't too tidy.

Most if not all of the garden tasks mentioned above can be left until spring, and more often than not this is the path I go down on the bigger tasks. However, there are some essentials that should be handled before the winter hiatus, to prevent disease and damage over the cold months to come.

Autumn garden tasks

Here are some jobs that are well worth tackling this autumn to keep shrubs and plants healthy, and the garden happy as the dormant season approaches.

1. Collect fallen leaves

It's particularly important to collect leaves from lawn areas, as wet leaves can smother the grass. Rake and gather leaves, either bagging them up or creating a pile in a protected spot, where they can decompose over the next year. Leaf mould or mulch is a good soil conditioner and weed suppressor. Best of all, it's free.

2. Order spring-flowering bulbs

While your borders still have structure, it's a good idea to assess the gaps and order your bulbs.

3. Tidy up

Clear plant matter from kitchen-garden beds and add it to the compost pile before it breaks down. This can help prevent disease from spreading if tackled promptly. Pull spent, soggy annuals from borders and add to the compost pile. Dismantle teepee structures and place them somewhere dry and well ventilated over the winter.

4. Tackle the weeds

Weeds will still be actively growing during the autumn months, although at a slower rate. Now is a good time to keep up your weeding routine. I usually stop pulling weeds after the first frosts, unless warm temperatures push active growth.

5. Plant

Plant out hardy biennials like foxgloves at least 6 weeks before the first frost, to allow them time to root in.

6. Prune

Lightly prune shrubs and hedges. Choose a dry day, then with clean shears tidy up any straggly new growth from over the summer.

7. Harvest

Dig up your potatoes, and place them to cure somewhere dry, warm and dark. (See page 105 for details.) Harvest pumpkins and cure them somewhere dry and sunny – this enables the skins to harden up and protect the flesh inside from deteriorating. (Place spent vines on the compost heap.)

8. Sow

Sow overwintering crops such as garlic, shallots and onions. (See page 133 for details.)

9. Leave dried seeds

Perennials that produce seedheads or that have dried in position can be left in place until the following spring, to provide food for wildlife and winter interest in the garden. They look particularly beautiful covered in cobwebs and dew or frost.

Bulbs, glorious bulbs

There is nothing quite like the arrival of autumn-planted bulbs the following spring. For the past few years I've taken to planting the majority of my bulb haul in pots, so I can move the colour around the garden to where it's needed, to line pathways, and of course for use in the plant-theatre displays. Here are my top tips for planting in pots.

YOU WILL NEED
- Frostproof pots
- Stones or crocks for each pot
- A gritty, multi-purpose, peat-free compost
- Bulbs (narcissus, tulip, muscari, hyacinth, iris, snowdrop, allium, crocus)
- Enough horticultural grit to top off your pots

METHOD
Add crocks
Place a layer of stones or crocks on the bottom of the pots, then fill around halfway with compost, leaving 7.5–12cm (3–5 inches) of space at the top.

Plant
Pop in your bulbs; I always plant them snugly, almost touching, with the pointy side facing up. Planting a single variety per pot adds to the impact and will hold its own among a larger display. Top the bulbs with another good layer of compost, leaving 2.5cm (1 inch) of space at the top of the pot.

Cover the soil
Add a layer of horticultural grit just to cover the soil. This helps with drainage, deters wildlife such as squirrels from stealing your bulbs, and I also think it looks rather smart. Water them in.

Shelter
Place somewhere sheltered from the worst of the winter weather. In particularly rainy climates, you could place your pots either in an unheated garage or shed, or cover them with a tarp. Do keep an eye on them, though, as they will need to be uncovered and brought out into the light as soon as the first shoots appear in early spring.

Some of my favourite spring-flowering bulb varieties

This is by no means an exhaustive list, but it does include some great options if you're looking for reliable naturalizing varieties.

GROUP	VARIETY
Alliums	Drumstick allium (*Allium sphaerocephalon*) *A.* 'White Empress' *A.* 'White Giant' – a large white sphere *A. schubertii* – looks like a sparkler or firework, and works beautifully dried
Crocus	*Crocus* 'Whitewell Purple' *C.* 'Firefly' Saffron crocus
Snowdrops	*Galanthus* 'Armine' – a taller variety *G.* 'Flore Pleno' – a delicate double *G. nivalis* – the most common snowdrop and an excellent naturalizer *G.* 'Primrose Warburg' – tipped with yellow on the inner blooms and ovary (the base of the flower) *G.* 'S. Arnott' – scented
White narcissi	*Narcissus* 'Bridal Crown' *N.* 'Horn of Plenty' *N.* 'Scilly White' *N.* 'Thalia'
Yellow narcissi	*Narcissus* 'February Gold' *N.* 'Yellow Cheerfulness' *N.* 'Hawera' *N.* 'Jetfire' *N.* 'Minnow' *N.* 'Tête-à-tête'
Iris	*Iris* 'Christmas Angel' – a stunning white variety perfect for a moon garden *I.* 'Katharine Hodgkin' – a delicate dwarf variety
Muscari	*Muscari azureum* – does well in sun or shade

Essential tips for bulbs

*If placed under cover, check your pots regularly for moisture,
and don't let them dry out completely.*

•

*Bulbs do need a period of cold in order to flower well,
at least 10–12 weeks, so planting between October
and late December is ideal.*

•

*Once foliage appears, fertilizing weekly will help your bulbs
to retain lots of energy to flower again the following year.
A potassium-focused feed is best.*

•

*Planting bulbs en masse across a lawn or border not only
makes for a dramatic display from later winter onwards to
spring, the early flowers also provide much-needed food for
early rising bees. The planting stage can be a time-consuming
endeavour, but after the first year nature will lend a helping
hand in growing your display, and you'll reap
the rewards for many years to come.*

Autumn-sown vegetables

Growing in autumn and overwintering vegetables and flowers for me personally is about finding a happy medium between getting a head start on next year's growing season and allowing the soil – and me – to rest over the winter months.

That said, there are a few vegetables I will sow in autumn without fail; those that are reliable, have proven to produce better and earlier crops when sown in the autumn, and require little to no input from me over the coldest months.

The best type of soil to plant both garlic and onions into is well-draining, loose and richly fertile soil. If you can easily push the garlic clove in with your hand, your onions and garlic will be able to bulb up easily over the long growing season. Before planting any crops, I top the beds with a few inches of fresh compost to add nutrients back into the soil.

Broad beans also do well if autumn sown. The earlier the crop, the less chance blackfly will develop on the plant. That said, affected leaves can be pinched off once the plant has started flowering.

TIP

Leave space between rows to sow companion plants with your alliums (garlic, shallots and onions) in the spring. Root vegetables such as carrots, celeriac and kale all make excellent companion plants.

Garlic

Separate the cloves in the bulb, leaving as much of the papery skin on each clove as possible. This helps to prevent rotting. I lay the bulbs on top of the soil around 10cm (4 inches) apart before planting to make sure I don't leave any gaps. Push the bulb pointy side up into the soil around 5cm (2 inches) deep and cover with soil.

Garlic varieties to try: Softneck – 'Iberian Wight' and 'Provence Wight'; Hardneck – 'Carcassonne Wight' and 'Caulk Wight'. Elephant garlic is a fun variety to grow, especially for children, as it forms a very large single bulb. It also has a milder taste than typical garlic varieties.

Shallots and onions

Plant bulbs, otherwise known as sets, with the skin on around 10cm (4 inches) apart. Push them into the soil until just the pointy tip remains above the surface. Cover with a mesh or cloche for a few weeks until they root in, to prevent birds from pulling them up.

Shallot varieties to try include 'Longor' for good storage life, and 'Zebrune'.

Broad beans

Sow the hardiest varieties of broad beans around 5cm (2 inches) deep and 10–15cm (4–6 inches) apart. They should germinate within a couple of weeks and will grow on happily over the winter months. Come spring, add stakes and string to support the beans as they grow. A couple of hardy and tasty varieties to try are 'Aquadulce Claudia' and 'The Sutton'. The 'Crimson Flowered' variety produces lovely dark pink flowers. If you encounter problems with autumn sowing, try sowing in pots first in the greenhouse before transplanting in spring, or start a spring crop in March.

Seasonal wreath

One of my favourite pastimes in the autumn and winter months is wreath-making. After gathering foliage and seedheads from the garden, along with dried flowers from bundles hung up indoors, I'll make a cup of tea and head to the potting shed with my garden treasures – often with no plan in mind, but with great ambition to make a beautiful piece of home decoration. Sometimes it works out well and sometimes I change course midway, but the process is always calming and very rewarding.

YOU WILL NEED
– Roll of twine or paddle wire (20- or 22-gauge wire works well)
– Scissors and snips
– A wreath form made from natural materials, such as willow (I used a 45cm/18 inch form)
– Gathered garden foliage (see over the page for ideas)
– Any extra adornments such as pine cones, dried fruit or dried poppy seedheads

METHOD

Wrap the wire around the top of the wreath form
3–4 times, leaving a few centimetres at the end to
twist around the wire still attached to the roll. Twist
to secure and set the wire to the side of the form.

Bunch together pieces of foliage of different textures
and lay them on the wreath form, facing slightly
towards the centre. Tightly wrap the wire around
the stems of the foliage three times, then set the
wire down.

Create another bundle and lay it on the form, slightly
overlapping the previous one to cover any visible
wire, this time facing outwards. Tightly wrap the wire
around the next bundle three times, then set the
wire down.

Repeat the steps until the wreath is complete. After
wrapping the final bundle with wire, cut the wire
leaving a length of around 25cm (10 inches) to feed
through the wreath a few times and secure it in place.
Wire on any extra adornments to finish.

TIPS

- *Don't cut the wire or twine until right at the end of the wreath-making process.*

- *Wrap each bundle tightly against the wreath form, because when they dry they shrink in size and can become loose.*

- *The size of each bundle determines the size of the wreath, so keep that in mind when deciding on the finished size you are planning.*

SEASONAL FOLIAGE AND FLOWER SUGGESTIONS

Autumn

Sedum heads, laurel, cotinus, hypericum, Astrantia 'Roma', pine cones, poppy seedheads and dried grasses

Winter

Berry stems, eucalyptus, pine cones, spruce or fir stems, holly, ivy

Spring

Forsythia, moss, muscari, dwarf narcissi, rosemary, dried heather, alpines such as saxifrage

Summer

Ivy, lavender, dried lemons, fennel, achillea, hydrangeas, strawflowers, scabious, astrantia

Creating an autumn porch display

Welcoming others to my home in autumn feels like a celebration all on its own. A mini harvest festival, if you will. Using my own home-grown pumpkins and squash gives a real sense of achievement. And if my crop of pumpkins isn't up to scratch, the family and I pile into the car and head off pumpkin-picking at our local patch. Either way, it's a fun way to usher in the new season.

The pumpkins and squash end up in the cold store if the temperatures look like they are going to dip below freezing, so we can enjoy them over the winter months. Anything that is past its best makes excellent foraging food for squirrels if hung up from a tree branch. Deer, foxes and badgers love them too!

CHRYSANTHEMUM TIPS

- *'Spray' chrysanthemums are readily found at garden centres in the autumn. If you're including them in an arrangement, choose plants with the buds still mostly closed to enjoy the flowers for longer.*

- *Taller cut-flower varieties are worth overwintering in a frost-free location to be planted out the following spring.*

- *Fertilize with a feed rich in potassium while blooming, to lengthen the display.*

The autumn garden

Creating a cold store

Creating additional space for food storage became a satisfying necessity during my fourth year of growing. After effectively doubling our growing space with the addition of the potager, I needed to find a home for the extra produce before the first frosts came around. Some root vegetables can remain in the ground over the colder months, to be pulled up and used as needed – carrots, potatoes and parsnips, to name a few – but living in an area that can see continual rain for weeks at a time, I much prefer to pull and store root crops, among other things, in a more controlled environment. This means we get the longest storage time possible and it avoids the risk of crops rotting in soggy ground or becoming food for worms.

To create a cold store, you'll need to choose a place that is dry, well-ventilated and away from direct sunlight. An outbuilding, garage or even an unheated porch has the potential to become a good option for long-term food storage. The aim is to create a refrigerator-type of climate as naturally as possible; an area that doesn't freeze, has good air flow and humidity, and is kept mostly free of light.

My cold store, or above-ground root cellar, if you prefer, started life as a humble shed with windows along one side. To convert it, I used leftover foam board insulation from a home renovation project placed between the frame of the internal walls, floor and ceiling, followed by lengths of sarking (long, rough-cut planks of softwood timber) laid horizontally on top, shiplap style, then nailed into place. I then gave it a light sand and a few coats of paint.

Installing a small vent in one wall ensured the air would flow well and prevent any buildup of ethylene, which can speed up the maturing process in crops and mean you need to eat through the produce quicker! Just make sure you cover the vent with a fine wire mesh to stop rodents getting in. Along with good air circulation, moderate to high humidity is a must. In Scotland, a country with consistent – scratch that, almost constant – rainfall, reaching a high humidity level is easy and rarely something I think about. Although I did pick up a thermometer for the cold store that had a built-in humidity detector, just to make sure. Between 75 and 90 per cent humidity is a good target to prevent most crops from wilting or drying out.

Andrew made simple wood shutters that could be placed over the windows to rest on a lip of wood nailed to the window frame. If you're storing potatoes, making sure they remain in the dark is essential to preventing them from turning green (which makes them toxic to eat) and rotting prematurely. For everything else, as little light as possible will stop your lovingly grown produce from sprouting early.

Dahlia tubers and apples are wrapped individually in newspaper and stored in crates. Pumpkins are placed on shelves lined with hessian. Potatoes are stored in kilo-sized hessian sacks or purpose-built potato baskets. Garlic bulbs and shallots are braided and hung from hooks, alongside flowers and chillies picked for drying. Carrots, parsnips and beetroot can be laid in between layers of damp sand; just make sure they are not touching.

To get the best from your produce, don't wash it until you're ready to use it. Winter squashes, onions and garlic benefit from curing before being placed in storage. Check everything regularly; I aim for around twice per month to make sure any spoilt crops are removed promptly so they don't affect any neighbouring produce.

In extreme winters, the cold store may struggle to remain above freezing, especially if it's a wooden structure such as a shed. To combat this, keep a roll of horticultural fleece or hessian handy to cover or line storage crates for extra insulation. Lining crates with 10cm (4 inches) of sawdust or newspaper also provides good insulation while letting air circulate.

It can be difficult to give all produce their individual perfect conditions, so I aim for a happy medium as much as possible. For the produce I generally store this means a temperature of around 3–5°C, (37–41°F) and 80 per cent humidity, which is the average for my area. I recommend researching the perfect storing temperature and humidity for what you grow and making a table that can be placed in your cold store as a reference guide.

As time has gone on, I've discovered more and more uses for this space – extra drinks storage for over the festive period, temporarily housing bulbs before planting time, and it's a great spot for keeping homemade preserves and chutneys. To maximize space vertical storage is key; repurposing milk or vegetable crates from a local farmer friend or grocer makes for excellent stackable storage that allows air to circulate easily throughout. I also use the cold store as a place to potter in early spring. The insulation keeps it warm enough for wreath-making or sowing an early batch of sweet peas. I'll crack open the shutters for a couple of hours and retreat inside with a cup of tea.

Calendula balm

Calendula balm is a true gift for a gardener's hands, with its anti-bacterial, anti-fungal and potent healing properties. It's a completely natural balm that works wonders for extremely dry skin, eczema, rashes, bites and scarring. I use this on my lips, hands and body throughout the winter months especially – well, when I can find it, as more often than not my husband will sneak off with my jar after finishing his own.

The recipe quantities here can be doubled if you need extra batches. You need to start the preparation for this over the summer, by snipping and gathering calendula flower heads throughout the growing season. The best time to pick them is while in peak bloom, then lay them flat on a sheet of baking paper indoors until they have dried completely – this usually takes around a week or two – and store in an airtight container until you have gathered enough.

YOU WILL NEED

- 4 large mason jars
- 3 large handfuls dried calendula flower heads
- 1 litre (1¾ pints) organic jojoba oil, or olive, almond or rapeseed oil
- 28g (1oz) beeswax in block or pastille form
- 1 tbsp shea butter
- 5–10 drops of essential oil (optional); my favourites are lavender and eucalyptus
- Clean jars with lids or lip-salve tins in your preferred size

METHOD

First make the infused oil. Choose a carrier oil. I love to use organic jojoba oil, but olive oil, almond oil or even rapeseed oil all work very well. Fill four 500ml (17fl oz) mason jars with the dried petals and fill to the top with the carrier oil (you'll need about 250ml/8½fl oz per jar). Leave the oil to infuse with the calendula flowers for around 6–8 weeks in a cool spot indoors, out of direct light. I have been known to forget about the jars infusing in my kitchen for months, which only benefits the infusion.

Place a bowl over a pot of simmering water, making sure the bowl does not touch the water, then add the infused oil, beeswax and shea butter. Stir occasionally and allow the beeswax to melt fully. Once completely combined, remove from the heat. Once off the heat, add the essential oil, if using, and stir to combine.

Pour into sterilized jars (see page 151 for details) and allow to set fully before screwing a lid onto each jar. They will store for up to a year in a cool dark place.

Butternut and Prosciutto Salad

My husband Andrew and I discovered this recipe while attending an Italian-themed cookery class in Johannesburg. It became a firm year-round favourite in our home, the perfect dish to serve when entertaining. It's always gone first! Little did we know that we would be making this recipe years later with squash and lettuces from our own garden.

It is the perfect recipe for those early autumn days when you're still clinging on to the last of summer, but also need the comforting food often associated with the turn of the season.

Serves 4 as
a main or
6 as a side

1 tsp coriander seeds
1 tsp ground cumin
1 dried chilli
1 tsp salt
1 tsp pepper
1 medium-sized winter squash (butternut, crown prince, uchiki kuri or whichever you prefer) peeled and cut into 2.5cm (1-inch) cubes
Olive oil, for drizzling
120g or 4 large handfuls of lamb's lettuce, rocket or mixed salad leaves
10–15 slices of prosciutto
60g (2oz) pine nuts
Parmesan shavings, to serve
Balsamic glaze, to drizzle

Preheat the oven to 180°C/160°C fan/350°F/gas mark 4.

Place the coriander seeds, cumin, chilli, salt and pepper in a pestle and mortar and grind together. In an ovenproof dish, place the cubed squash and drizzle with a good glug of olive oil. Rub the squash with the olive oil until all the pieces are covered, then sprinkle with the spice mix and shake the tray until evenly coated. Roast in the oven for around 30–40 minutes until the squash is golden and soft. Set aside to cool slightly.

On a platter arrange the lamb's lettuce, slices of prosciutto and squash. (It doesn't have to be neat.)

In a dry pan, gently toast the pine nuts on a medium heat until they just begin to colour. Sprinkle over the salad, and top with shavings of Parmesan. Last but not least, drizzle with balsamic glaze before serving.

Any-colour-goes Tomato Chutney

At the end of my first year growing tomatoes I had a harvest basket full of mostly unripened fruits and no clue what to do with them. As I pondered the options, the early 90s movie *Fried Green Tomatoes* popped into my head and I knew there must be an abundance of recipes for green tomatoes to try. I've tested a few over the years including fried, relished and cooked down for soup, but this one for chutney, tweaked over the last couple of years, is still the firm favourite.

Makes approx.
5 x 400ml
(13½fl oz) jars

4 tbsp olive oil
1kg (2¼lb) yellow onions, chopped
1 tbsp mixed spice
1 heaped tsp yellow mustard seeds
1 small red chilli, chopped and deseeded or not,
   depending on how spicy you like it!
2 bay leaves
6 garlic cloves, finely chopped
2kg (4½lb) mix of green, red, yellow, purple tomatoes
   – whatever you have, chopped roughly
500g (1lb 2oz) cooking apples, peeled and diced
700ml (1¼ pints) apple cider vinegar
1 tbsp salt
400g (14oz) light soft brown sugar
200g (7oz) dates, pitted and chopped
200g (7oz) sultanas

Heat the oil in a deep, heavy-based pan, then gently cook the onions until soft and translucent. Add the spices, bay leaves and garlic and cook for a further 5–8 minutes. Next add the tomatoes, apples and around half of the apple cider vinegar. Simmer on a medium heat for 10–15 minutes until the tomatoes and apples have softened.

Pour in the remainder of the apple cider vinegar, then add the salt, sugar, dates and sultanas, and cook very gently until the sugar dissolves. Once dissolved, turn the heat up a touch, and simmer the chutney for 1–2 hours. Tomatoes with a higher water content may take longer to reduce down. The chutney should be a thick consistency at this point, almost like jam. Be careful at this stage, as it is easy for the sugar to burn on the bottom of the pan. Turn off the heat and remove the bay leaves.

I use glass jars with glass lids and rubber seals to store my chutney. I always opt for a small-sized jar, so that once the seal is broken the chutney can be used relatively quickly. Sterilize the jars and any utensils you may be using by washing them in hot soapy water and rinsing well, then dry them thoroughly in the oven at a temperature of around 160°C/140°C fan/320°F/gas mark 3 for 10–15 minutes.

Carefully spoon the chutney into the warm jars and add the lids. The chutney is ready to eat once cooled, but it can be left to mature for a few weeks first. I store mine unopened in a cupboard for up to 6 months. Once opened I store it in the fridge and eat with 4 weeks.

Andrew's Fresh Chilli Relish

This is a wonderful way to preserve a glut of chillies. It makes the perfect spice rub or marinade for meat or fish and you can use it in wraps or salads, or even add a spoon to pasta sauces for a kick. Or you can do what Andrew does and have it as a condiment with every meal!

Makes approx.
2 x 250ml
(8½fl oz) jars

400g (14oz) mixed chillies (whatever you're growing, removing the seeds will reduce the spice level)
Thumb-size piece of ginger (optional)
6 garlic cloves (optional)
50ml (2fl oz) red wine vinegar
Roughly 100ml (3½fl oz) olive oil or until you get the consistency of a Greek yoghurt
Juice of ½ lemon
Good pinch of salt

Roughly chop the chillies. Peel and roughly chop the ginger and garlic. Put everything in a blender. Add the vinegar and half of the olive oil, then blend until all ingredients are well combined. Add the remaining olive oil, or as much as required to get the right consistency, and blitz again. Add the lemon juice and salt to taste. Give it one last blitz.

Decant into a sterilized airtight container (see page 151 for how to sterilize). Andrew will usually split the relish between two jars – keeping one for us and giving one to my mum, who also loves chillies.

This will store in the fridge for up to four weeks. The flavour intensifies as time goes on. Top the relish with olive oil as needed to keep the flavour less ardent.

My Mum's
End-of-the-week Veggie Bake

This is not an exact-science recipe but more of an experiment with what you have, as it really depends on what's on hand in the garden and in the fridge. Lots of different vegetables will work. Broccoli, cauliflower, carrots and parsnips are all good here, but avoid using soft vegetables such as courgettes. If you don't have shallots, onion or leeks are good substitutes. For the cheese sauce, any hard cheese will do, such as Cheddar, Stilton or Parmesan.

Serves 4–5

About 800g (1¾lb) vegetables, cut into 2.5–5cm (1–2 inch) cubes
1–2 garlic cloves, finely chopped
1–2 shallots, diced
1–2 handfuls of cheeses, grated or crumbled
570ml (20fl oz) single cream (see note in recipe)
Enough potatoes for topping the dish, peeled and evenly sliced about 1cm (⅜ inch) thick
Salt and black pepper, to taste

Preheat the oven to 180°C/160°C fan/350°F/gas mark 4.

Place the veg in a baking dish approximately 20–30cm (8–12 inches), and add the garlic, shallots, a grind or two of pepper and only a small pinch of salt, as the cheeses will add to the salt.

Mix most of the grated cheese in a large bowl and add the cream. (The quantity of cream specified works with the suggested size of baking dish; adjust as needed.) Mix well and pour over the vegetables. Use a spoon to make sure the sauce is evenly distributed. Place a layer of sliced potatoes on top. Sprinkle with a pinch of salt.

Cover with tin foil and bake in the oven for 20 minutes. After 20 minutes, remove the foil, add a grating of hard cheese on top and cook until golden brown. My mum recommends enjoying with crusty bread and a fine red wine!

Winter

Winter renewal

The stillness of winter feels like a gift from nature after three active seasons in the garden, an acknowledgement that the natural world has paused and it's all right for me to do the same.

Winter is often a season filled with reflection and days of hibernation as the year comes to an end, both of which I revel in to a degree. At the same time, I love the creativity and renewed homemaker-energy that the season inspires within me.

Since becoming a gardener, I now look for ways to continue to connect with nature in some form or another over the winter, whether that's creating foraged arrangements, collecting home-grown produce from the cold store to make hearty meals, taking long rambling walks, or just staring out of the window watching fat snowflakes fall. There is enjoyment for the gardener in every season, not just those in which seeds are sown.

Decorating for the festive season has always brought me joy. The look on my children's faces when they first see the twinkly lights or garlands draped along the stairs, and stockings in place over the mantel, is priceless and precious. These days, natural elements make up the centrepieces of my decor, with garlands made from fir boughs, eucalyptus and dried oranges for colour and scent and a potted Christmas tree in the dining room that will be planted out in the garden once the season has passed.

However, before we reach the festive season and can down tools for a while, there are still a few jobs to complete outside before the garden nods off to sleep.

Early winter garden tasks

Here are a few garden tasks to tackle on a 'fresh' winter's day.

1. Plant last bulbs

Plant any remaining bulbs into pots or the ground. Tulips in particular do better with a later planting. I aim for around November to get these in the ground, as long as the soil is workable, because tulips need to be planted fairly deep. Between 15–20cm (6–8 inches) is ideal.

2. Remove older leaves and foliage

Remove any yellowing or wilted foliage from around winter crops such as Brussels sprouts, cabbage or sprouting broccoli. This will ensure enough air is getting to the plant and will help it to direct its energy to maturing the rest of the crop.

3. Plant hedges

Between November and February is the best time to plant new hedging, as it will be available to buy in the more economical bare-root form – where it arrives without a pot, with just the roots. Whether you plant these out in a row in a trench or singly, adding mycorrhizal fungi to the planting hole will help the hedging roots establish quickly.

4. Check for snow damage

After a heavy snowfall, check trees and shrubs and shake off the snow to prevent damage to the plants, such as broken branches.

5. Mulch

Mulch around any half-hardy plants that may need a little more protection to make it through the winter. In my area this includes asparagus and artichokes. A layer of straw or compost will offer a little blanket of warmth against the worst of the weather.

6. Clear paths

Remove moss, leaves and residue buildup from patios and pathways with a stiff brush or power washer to prevent them turning into an ice rink as the temperature drops.

The early
winter garden

Winter sowing method

I first discovered the winter sowing method on the Garden Answer YouTube channel. It intrigued me, as it's a fully hands-off growing process that relies solely on light, moisture and heat to trigger germination and ongoing growth. This is a great method to try if you don't have a greenhouse or indoor growing setup, and if your growing ambitions exceed your current indoor growing space! It's also the perfect job to tackle midwinter, if you're just itching to get some seeds sown. January to mid-February is a good time to get sowing.

YOU WILL NEED
- 2-litre (3½-pint) jugs, rinsed and lids removed (such as milk containers)
- Stanley knife
- Multi-purpose compost
- Perlite, vermiculite or horticultural grit
- Garden marker pen
- Small roll of electrical or duct tape
- Labels

METHOD

Start by carefully piercing 6–8 holes into the bottom of each jug with the knife. Then use the knife to slice round the centre of the jug, leaving around 2.5cm (1 inch) of uncut centre on the handle side to create a hinge.

Mix 3 parts multi-purpose compost with 1 part perlite, vermiculite or horticultural grit to create a free-draining compost. Fill the bottom half of the jug with the mix up to 2.5cm (1 inch) below the cut centre. Sow the seeds according to the seed packet and top with a fine layer of vermiculite to help the mix retain moisture.

Water in your seeds, and label before closing the lid. Secure the lid closed with the electrical tape, wrapped twice around, and write the variety on the jug with the garden marker.

Place your jugs somewhere that gets lots of sun and rain, avoiding any very windy areas. Once your seeds have germinated in early spring, open the lids during the day and close them overnight as you would the greenhouse. If your area receives consistent rainfall or snow over the winter months you shouldn't need to water them. However, do check them every once in a while to make sure.

Seeds that require a period of stratification (cold temperatures) to germinate are perfect for sowing with this method. It also works well with flowers such as larkspur, poppies, foxgloves, calendula, verbascums, violas, snapdragons and delphiniums, as well as vegetables including lettuce, kale, broccoli, cauliflower, chard, cabbage, spinach and beetroot.

Sweet peas

One of the jewels of the early summer garden, these delicate beauties are the perfect accompaniment to add colour to the kitchen garden, or to turn a drab courtyard wall into a sweet-scented summer display. A few in a collection of bud vases down the centre of a table make for a simple yet effective centrepiece at a summer barbecue.

YOU WILL NEED
- Sweet pea seeds
- 9cm (3½ inch) pots, empty toilet rolls or purpose-made root trainers (sweet peas have a fast-growing root system that needs a deeper container to thrive well in)
- A propagator lid (usually this comes as part of the set; if not, a piece of bubble wrap secured with elastic over the top of a pot does the same thing)
- Peat-free multi-purpose compost
- Labels and a garden marker pen

METHOD
Soak the seeds in water for up to 24 hours prior to sowing – you will need 2 seeds per root trainer cell or 2–3 seeds per 9cm (3½ inch) pot. Seeds should be sown 1cm (½ inch) below the soil, covered over with more compost and watered in well. Pop the label in and the lid on, and if sown in autumn (at least six weeks before the first frost) place in the greenhouse to germinate and grow slowly over the winter. If sown in late winter, around the end of January to the middle of March, let them germinate in the warmth of the house. As soon as they appear, move the seedlings back out to the greenhouse to grow on. Sweet peas need lots of light and cooler temperatures to get a strong start.

Keep the seedlings moist at all times. Once around 10–15cm (4–6 inches) tall, pinch off the top set of leaves to help the seedling thicken and branch out.

Sweet peas may survive a few cold nights and a light frost, as a hardy annual, but in order to do so they should be hardened off thoroughly before planting out. As they are not keen on root disturbance, plan to plant out the whole cell together when you get to that stage. Plant into fertile soil, adding an obelisk or trellis structure for them to climb up.

As they climb, tie them in at regular intervals with a piece of twine, and keep them well watered. Feed weekly with a high-potash fertilizer such as a seaweed or tomato feed, then pick the blooms regularly to encourage further flowers and prevent the plant from going to seed too soon.

At the end of the flowering period, the plants will set seeds that look like pea pods, although these are not edible. Leave them on the plant until dry, then pop the seeds into a labelled envelope to store in your seed tin for sowing the following autumn.

Winter cutting garden

In the run up to the festive season, the process of foraging from the garden to create seasonal decorations has become a much-loved tradition. I look forward to bundling up and venturing out with my secateurs and a bucket to gather vibrant evergreens in varying shades and textures, berry-laden stems and handfuls of moss to act as a base for my creations. As the years have gone by, I've added more winter interest to the garden and my own winter cutting bed of sorts, which I use to make wreaths, garlands and table centrepieces.

These are my must-have perennials for an abundant winter cutting garden.
- Blue Maid holly (*Ilex* x *meserveae*)
- Dogwood (*Cornus alba*)
- *Eucalyptus gunnii*
- Hellebores
- *Hypericum* 'Hidcote'
- Nordmann fir
- Norway spruce
- Pussy willow
- Scots pine
- *Skimmia japonica*
- Variegated ivy
- Winterberry holly (*Ilex verticillata*)

Winter-brightening indoor arrangements

Fresh home-grown flowers in the depths of winter are definitely one of life's little luxuries, and having them to hand is easily achievable if you choose the right flowers to grow. Paperwhites are one such flower – they are part of the *Narcissus* family, but as they originate from the Mediterranean they don't require a long cold period to bloom successfully like other daffodil varieties do. I like to buy a bag of 'Paperwhite Ziva' bulbs, as I love the stronger sweet scent that in recent years has become synonymous with the festive season in my home. However, if you prefer something more subtle, try 'Paperwhite Inbal' instead. Paperwhites are not in the slightest bit fussy and can be grown in a variety of mediums – compost, gravel or glass pebbles. They look just as beautiful grown inside a tall glass vase as they do in a wicker basket surrounded by moss and twigs.

YOU WILL NEED

- A container – terracotta or ceramic pots, wicker trays or even a jug will work
- Growing medium of your choice
- Paperwhite bulbs (usually available to purchase from autumn onwards)
- Other seasonal foliage such as moss, pine cones and twigs

METHOD

Fill your pot three-quarters deep with your growing medium, then nestle the bulbs about a third of the way into it, pointy side up. Placing the bulbs closely together will create more impact. Top up with the growing medium to cover the bulbs. Add a little water and place them somewhere cool to begin with, such as a porch or greenhouse.

Once you start to see growth, move them to a lighter and warmer location. If it's too warm or dark the stems will grow too quickly and may become floppy, so positioning them near a bright window, away from a heat source like an open fire or radiator, is best. If needed, you can provide them with support in the form of a cane. Water regularly so they don't dry out.

From planting to blooming takes around 4–6 weeks, so you need to plan ahead a bit. It's become a fun challenge each year to see if I can time them correctly for blooms on Christmas Day.

Immune-boosting Chicken
with Tomatoes and Garlic

Garlic is known to have a whole host of health benefits, including boosting the immune system, lowering cholesterol and reducing the risk of certain types of cancers. When the cold and flu season comes round, I love to make this recipe for the family to enjoy and get an immunity boost! There is a lot of garlic in this recipe, but roasting the garlic sweetens and softens the flavour profile, and home-grown roasted garlic is simply delicious.

Serves 6

Olive oil, for frying
6–8 organic chicken legs or thighs
120ml (4fl oz) white wine
14 fresh Roma tomatoes blitzed in a blender or
   600g (1lb 5oz) tinned tomatoes
2 tbsp tomato paste
10–12 garlic cloves, peeled
A small bunch of fresh herbs (I use a mix of oregano,
   sage, parsley and basil)
Salt and black pepper, to taste
Cooked pasta, to serve
Grated Parmesan, to serve

Preheat the oven to 190°C/170°C fan/375°F/gas mark 5.

In a Dutch oven or heavy-based ovenproof pan, add a drizzle of olive oil. Season the chicken with salt and pepper, then brown for a few minutes on both sides over a high heat, before removing from the pan with tongs and setting to one side.

Add the wine to the pan and cook for a minute or so to reduce slightly. Add the tomatoes to the pan, along with the tomato paste and simmer for around 10 minutes. Take off the heat. Place the browned chicken pieces back into the pan and scatter the whole cloves of garlic and the herbs over the top, using the tongs to submerge them in the sauce. Pop the lid on and cook for 1 hour in the oven.

Check the seasoning and serve over al dente conchiglie, macaroni or fusilli pasta, and finish with a handful of freshly grated Parmesan.

Winter Warmer Thai-style Soup

I first discovered this recipe online when my children were little, and since then I've made it countless times in every season, but there is just something about having this hearty soup in the middle of winter that creates a sense of warmth and wellbeing as the coconutty aroma fills the kitchen. Since I first made this, I've tweaked the recipe somewhat, but it's still a quick and simple soup with a lovely depth of flavour.

Serves 4

1 tbsp olive oil
150g (5oz) white onion, finely chopped
1 garlic clove, finely chopped
1 red chilli, finely chopped (remove the seeds
  for a milder heat)
600ml (20fl oz) chicken stock
300ml (10fl oz) coconut milk
2 organic chicken breasts, cut into thin strips
200g (7oz) broccoli florets
150g (5oz) cooked wild rice
Salt and black pepper, to season

Heat the oil in a pot over a medium heat and sauté the onion, garlic and chilli for a few minutes but don't let them brown. Pour in the chicken stock and coconut milk, turn up the heat and bring to the boil.

Add the chicken and broccoli to the pot and turn down the heat. Simmer for around 6–8 minutes until the chicken is cooked and the broccoli is tender but still has a little bite to it. Add the cooked rice and stir through to heat.

Season to taste and serve, making sure each bowl has a good mix of broth, chicken, broccoli and rice.

Late winter
garden tasks

Here are some garden tasks to get you outdoors, when you're craving a bracing winter's day.

1. Care for the birds
By late winter there is a lot less available in hedgerows and shrubs for foraging birds, so keep bird feeders topped up. To prevent the spread of disease, wash the bird feeders in a bucket of hot soapy water and dry thoroughly before refilling. Regularly check the bird bath has water, removing any large chunks of ice and topping up with fresh water as needed.

2. Prune roses
Around February or March is a good time to prune shrub roses, just as they break dormancy. Pick a dry day and with clean pruners remove any dead, damaged, diseased or crossing stems – you are aiming for an open shape and even trim.

3. Rest
Although there are other garden jobs that could be tackled in late winter – for example pruning fruit trees, working on hard landscaping projects or clearing up herbaceous borders – sometimes the pleasure in gardening is knowing when to stop. When to rest and let your garden rest too. When to let nature take hold and run its natural course for a little while longer before the garden rises again for spring.

If you're craving a floral fix or a way to feel a connection with nature during the depths of winter, why not try one of the following:
– Make a wreath using the dried flowers gathered throughout the season.
– Create a foraged table centrepiece or arrangement to elevate a mealtime, just because.
– Enjoy breakfast around a campfire. On a still, bright winter day, porridge or sausages cooked over smouldering embers is an invigorating way to get some fresh air – especially with a mug of hot tea for company.
– Press some winter-blooming flowers to make art with. Cyclamens, snowdrops, hellebores, violas, winter aconites, ivy and crocus all make beautiful pressed flowers.

The late
winter garden

Looking Back

I do hope you have enjoyed our time together. As a family, we have made many wonderful memories over the years in which we've been lucky enough to call Greenfields home. We, like so many, have experienced extremely sad times too, as the harshness of life sometimes seeps under the door and takes hold. Yet I hope this book has brought you some moments of peace through the imagery and inspired you to have a go at creating your own garden sanctuary. I hope it has given you confidence and that you now realize all the skills you need can be self-taught. As someone whose gardening experience once amounted to growing watercress at primary school, if I can do it anyone can!

With all the uncertainty in the world and life's constant twists and turns, I feel it's more important now than ever to be versatile, adaptable, to be open to change, to try to add more strings to our bows, so to speak.

If you're already growing at home, I hope you have been able to soak up the achievement of growing, cooking and creating with your own produce and flowers. Lastly, and most important of all, I hope you have been able to slow down and revel in the beauty of the seasons and all that they have to offer.

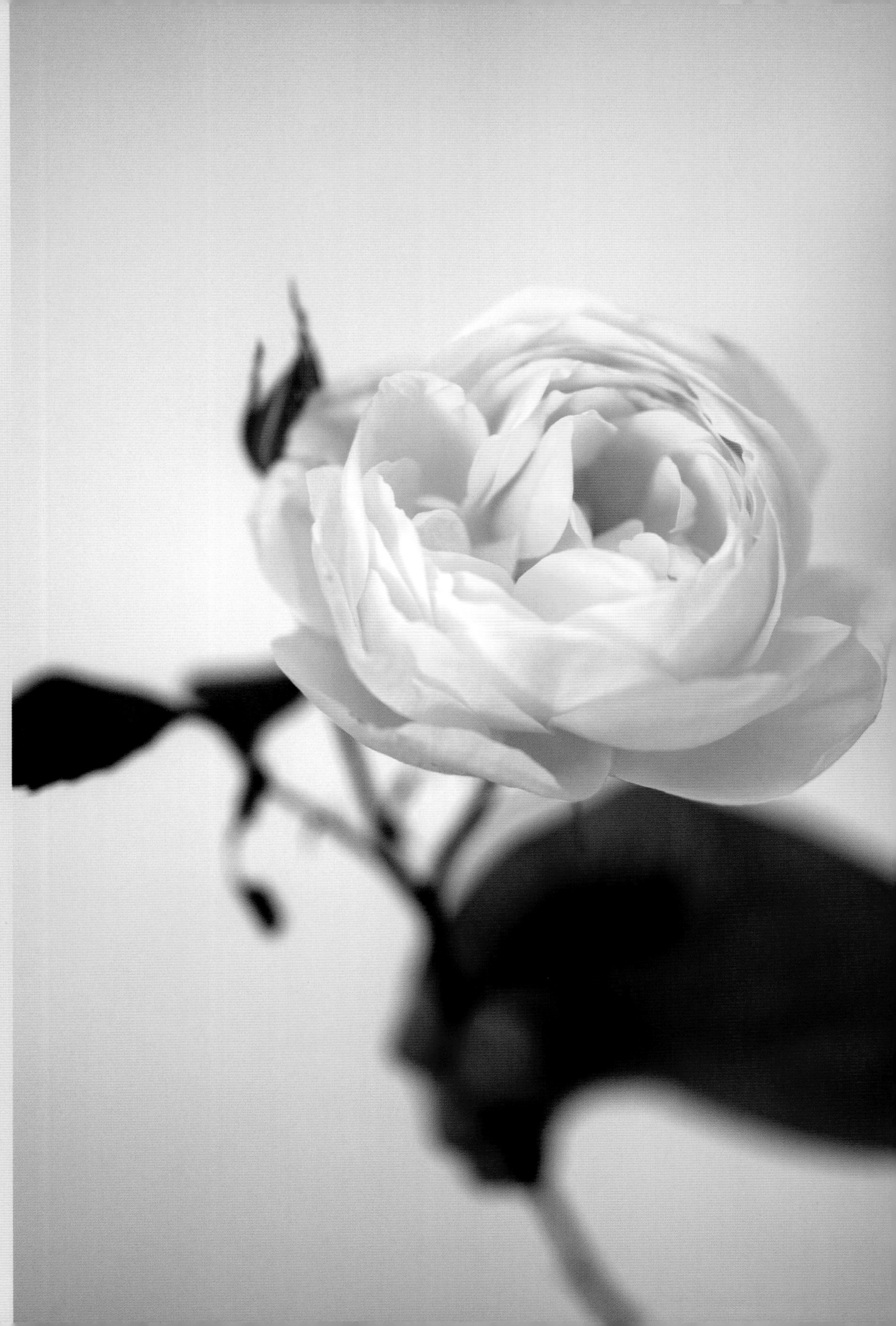

Afterword

Saying the journey to writing this book has not been easy would be the understatement of the decade. Every area of my life was imploding during the 18-month project. Within my family, we were collectively coping with anxiety, grief, PTSD and depression after losing Joseph, just trying to get through the first year without him. Family counselling and individual therapy was relied upon heavily to get us from week to week.

Andrew and I were under major strain financially, and the very night before the first order from his new business came in, we had decided to put Greenfields on the market – it was that close to the wire. It would have happened long before without the help received from both of our families, and for their support we are eternally grateful.

With bouts of insomnia and almost zero concentration, I would often go weeks without writing a thing, nor achieve much everywhere else in my life. My mum would come over to help me with curtain orders when restrictions allowed, just to help me get through the day.

The one thing that kept coming back to me was the promise I made to Joseph at his funeral. He was an extraordinary little boy, who always said yes to getting involved, learning and trying new things. I could write a book about his very special story. Suffice to say, he lived his life to the max. Every. Single. Day. I promised him I would do the same in an effort to be extraordinary just like him, and his two big sisters. My three musketeers... I would no longer let opportunities pass me by out of fear; from then on, the only answer would be yes.

Since then the power of saying yes has opened many doors, including appearing on the Scotland-based gardening programme *Beechgrove*. A show I distinctly remember watching as a little girl, who at the time had no interest in gardening. Surreal!

continues...

Since then I've continued to say yes to those life-affirming opportunities, to things that scare me but at the same time make me happy and fulfilled. It's fair to say that *Growing at Greenfields* is not just a book about growing vegetables and flowers, it's the story of personal growth that trying something new took me on, and held me steady through so much change and loss. I can only hope this book inspires you to take the leap and to strive for what makes your heart sing with joy.

To Andrew, my biggest cheerleader. How grateful I am to walk this life with you. Thank you for always helping with all my harebrained ideas, for always being in my corner, and for listening to my read-throughs countless times.

To Mia, my girl with the very old soul and the wicked sense of humour. How fortunate I am to experience your wisdom, kindness and wit every day. I continually learn from you. I am infinitely proud of all that you are. You go, glen coco.

To Georgia, you, my girl, are a force of light and positivity. I am continually in awe of how grounded and brave you are, and of the sheer talent and determination you possess. There is no one on Earth I would rather sing with than you. Well, maybe Celine, but I'm not sure if she practises every day. I may need to check... oh, wait.

Thank you both for your support while I hid away to write.

Common gardening terms

This is not a definitive list, but it does contain all specific gardening terms used within this book.

Annual A plant that from seed will grow, bloom, set seed and die within the same growing year.

Biennial A plant that blooms in its second year of growth before dying.

Chitting Forcing potatoes to sprout, in a bright, frost-free location for 4–6 weeks prior to planting.

Companion planting A method of planting crops or flowers together for mutual benefit, usually as a form of pest control.

Crop rotation Growing the same crop in different areas each year to prevent pests or disease.

Curing Drying vegetables for storage, usually to produce a protective layer of hardened or papery skin.

Deciduous Shrubs and trees that lose their leaves in winter.

Dormant When a plant is not actively growing, usually during the winter months.

Drill A narrow channel dug into the soil in which to sow seeds.

Early potatoes Also known as new potatoes or baby potatoes. A small tender variety of potato, grown and harvested early in the growing season. Not for storing due to its thin skin; a great boiling potato.

Evergreen Shrubs and trees that keep their leaves all year round.

First frost The first time in autumn where the temperature dips below 0°C (32°F).

Germination The point when the seed breaches the soil surface, and the first above-soil foliage is visible.

Half-hardy Plants that survive through cold temperatures but not a hard frost.

Hardening off Acclimatizing seedlings started off indoors to an outside environment.

Hardwood cuttings Older growth, usually taken during the dormant season from late autumn to midwinter.

Hardy A plant tough enough to survive winter in your area.

Last frost The last time in late spring when the temperature dips below 0°C (32°F).

Maincrop potatoes A larger forming potato, usually planted in spring and harvested in autumn. Maincrop potatoes store well and are versatile in the kitchen – can be mashed, roasted, boiled etc.

Mulch Homemade or shop-bought compost, bark or leaf mould. All can be used to protect plants, suppress weeds and retain moisture within the soil.

Perennial A plant that should return year after year.

Potting on Moving a seedling to a larger-size pot.

Pricking out Planting seedlings, usually started off together in one container, into individual pots.

Self-seeders Plants that spread by dropping seeds late in the growing season, which in turn grow new plants. Forget-me-nots, foxgloves, sunflowers and poppies all self-seed.

Softwood cuttings Flexible young growth, usually taken during the first half of the growing season.

Stratification The period of cold or warmth needed for some seeds to germinate.

Tender A plant unable to withstand winter temperature in your area. Usually native to a warmer climate. A tender perennial will return year after year, but will need protection over the winter months.

Thin out To remove smaller or weaker seedlings to allow space for remaining seedlings to grow on.

True leaves The true leaves are also known as the second set of leaves that grow on a seedling. The first set of leaves are called the cotyledons.

Tuber The underground part of the stem from which new plants emerge. Potatoes are grown from tubers known as seed potatoes. Dahlias are also grown from tubers.

Further reading

To continue to follow my journey of growing at Greenfields, find me here:
Instagram @Growing_Greenfields
www.growinggreenfields.co.uk

Books

The Almanac, Lia Leendertz
　　(Gaia, published annually)
Containers in the Garden, Claus Dalby
　　(Cool Springs Press, 2022)
Floret Farm's Cut Flower Garden, Erin Benzakein
　　(Chronicle Books, 2017)
Grow, Cook, Nourish, Darina Allen
　　(Kyle Books, 2017)
The Flower Yard, Arthur Parkinson
　　(Kyle Books, 2021)
How to Grow a Garden, Ellen Mary
　　(Greenfinch, 2022)
The Well Gardened Mind, Sue Stuart-Smith
　　(William Collins, 2021)

YouTube channels

Eugenia Diaz
Garden Answer
Huw Richards
Monalogue

My favourite gardeners and gardens on Instagram

SCOTLAND
Rachel, @gardenerscottageedinburgh
Katie Townsend, @katietownsendgardendesign
Julianne Robertson, @mycornerofearth
Suz Roberts, @scottishveggiegarden

ENGLAND
Terry Winters, @terrywinters9141
Kate Coulson, @katecoulson
Alex, @theenglishgardener
Stina, @thehackneygardener
Paula Sutton, @hillhousevintage
Irene, @irenemylife
Zoe Woodward, @zoewoodwardgardening
Debbie, @mrsbeesgarden
Charlie McCormick, @mccormickcharlie

AMERICA
Laura LeBoutillier, @gardenanswer
Laura, @howsitgrowinnj

CANADA
Emily, @emc.homeandgardendesign

DENMARK
@clausdalby

Thank you

Thank you to my lovely mum, my sister and best friend Bianca, my nephew and niece, Callaghan and Mckenzie – the best garden helpers I know – and my in-laws Stan and Sandra, for your unwavering support and encouragement. Thank you to the amazing team at Pavilion, Clare Double and Laura Russell in particular for guiding me through the whole new world of book-making, and for making me a beautiful book! To Zöe Barrie for capturing the garden so magically, who knew golden light on carrots could be so thrilling! What a joy it was to work with you. To my extended family and friends who made sure that even though my family grieved mostly in isolation we were never lonely: words are not enough. With special thanks to Dr Scott for picking up my family and getting us through the darkest days, and to Dr Baseotto for helping me work through the worst. Last but not least, to the Instagram community who connect with me daily, who share snippets of their lives and gardens from all over the world, you all are simply the best!

About the author

Diana Yates began her career in a fast-paced corporate supply chain and spent 10 years living and working in South Africa. In 2017, she and her family returned home to southern Scotland and bought Greenfields, an 18th-century listed former manse with two acres of land. Diana is now a regular presenter on the BBC gardening show *Beechgrove* and spends time every day developing her fruit and vegetable garden. She also runs a successful business making bespoke curtains, blinds and cushions. *Growing at Greenfields* is her first book.

Index

Pavilion
An imprint of HarperCollins*Publishers*
1 London Bridge Street
London SE1 9GF

www.harpercollins.co.uk

HarperCollins*Publishers*
Macken House
39/40 Mayor Street Upper
Dublin 1
D01 C9W8
Ireland

10 9 8 7 6 5 4 3 2 1

First published in Great Britain by Pavilion
An imprint of HarperCollins*Publishers* 2023

A catalogue record of this book is available from the British Library

ISBN 978-1-91168-250-9

Printed and bound in China by RR Donnelley APS

Publishing Director: Stephanie Milner
Commissioning Editor: Lucy Smith
Managing Editor: Clare Double
Editorial Assistant: Ellen Simmons
Design Manager: Laura Russell
Design: maru studio
Production Manager: Sarah Burke

Photographer: Zöe Barrie
Photographs on back cover and pages 14 (top), 17, 19, 28–29, 32–33, 53 (above and below
left), 58, 71, 82 (below right), 84, 128 (except below right), 161, 162, 163 (above left), 166,
168, 170, 185, 188–189 by Diana Yates
Illustrations on pages 12 and 13 by Jitesh Patel